HEART OF A WOMAN, MIND OF A WRITER, AND SOUL OF A POET

A Critical Analysis of the Writings of Maya Angelou

Lyman B. Hagen

University Press of America, Inc.
Lanham • New York • London

Copyright © 1997 by
University Press of America,® Inc.
4720 Boston Way
Lanham, Maryland 20706

3 Henrietta Street
London, WC2E 8LU England

Library of Congress Cataloging-in-Publication Data

Hagen, Lyman B.
Heart of a woman, mind of a writer, and soul of a poet : a critical
analysis of the writngs of Maya Angelou / Lyman B. Hagen.
p. cm.
Includes bibliographical references and index.
1. Angelou, Maya--Criticism and interpretation. 2. Women and
literature--United States--History--20th century. 3. Afro-American
women in literature. 4. Afro-American in literature. I. Title.
PS3551.N464Z68 1997   818'.5409--dc20   96-47119 CIP

ISBN 0-7618-0620-2 (cloth: alk. ppr.)
ISBN 0-7618-0621-0 (pbk: alk. ppr.)

Contents

Preface

Maya Angelou opened her life to public scrutiny through her works. She writes as a woman, an African American, and the mother of an African-American male. She speaks to her race's history as she experiences it and as it has been passed down to her. But while the color of her skin affects how she perceives and how she is perceived, it is not her central concern. She explores relationships and the reactions of human beings to one another and to the circumstances surrounding them. Angelou exudes a vitality and a positive outlook that is contagious. She has known depression, discouragement, and disappointment. But her message of survival rings clear--"And Still I Rise."

Literary criticism of African-American writing has grown considerably in very recent times. The growth has been in both quantity and quality. A new generation of academics has discovered the rich trove of their ethnic literature and is examining it from both established and newly formulated scholarly norms. In the process they are discovering the contributions and talents of their brothers and sisters. Maya Angelou is one of the popular writers whose books have been subjected to increasing analysis and found to contain depth and layers overlooked in hasty, though entertaining, reading. What follows is an attempt to present some of these layered perceptions and their derivation as presented throughout the breadth of an entire body of work. There is hopefully a fresh look at the humor, ethics, and folklore contained in these works.

The message and spirit conveyed by the writings of Maya Angelou and the public acceptance of her published corpus on both the academic and general levels establish her as an American author of significance. The purpose of this volume is to validate that thesis and to provide a single reference source for those wishing to look more closely at the eclectic offerings of Angelou.

A note about style. Whenever possible, the term African American has been employed. Many direct quotes, however, use the terminology black or Negro. To avoid awkwardness, some textual references follow this usage, especially when referring to ethnic entity. Sometimes African American has been labeled too inclusive a term. American natives of Haiti, or Jamaica, or West Indian extraction have stated a preference for their origin to be noted in referring to them: i.e. Haitian American; or Jamaican American; etc.

Acknowledgments

My exploration of the writings of Maya Angelou began with a brief biography written for an Arkansas Author series for the Arkansas Endowment for the Humanities.

Thanks are due to Arkansas State University for a period of released time allowing necessary research. The department of English and Philosophy is supportive of scholarly endeavor. The staff of the Dean B. Ellis Library of Arkansas State University helped in locating materials for me. Carol Johnson and Robin Joslin patiently prepared my manuscript for publication. I sincerely appreciate their efforts.

Grateful acknowledgment is made to:

Random House, Inc. for permission to print excerpts from *I Know Why the Caged Bird Sings*, copyright (c) 1969 by Maya Angelou and *Gather Together in My Name,* copyright (c) 1974 by Maya Angelou;

Claudia Tate for excerpts from *Black Women Writers at Work*, edited by Claudia Tate, (c) 1983 by Continuum;

Dutton, Inc. for permission to print excerpts from *Like It Is*, edited by Emily Rovetch. Copyright (c) 1981 by Central State University. Used by permission of Dutton Signet, a division of Penguin Books USA Inc.

Chronology

1928   Maya Angelou (Marguerite Johnson) born 4 April 1928 in St. Louis, Missouri, the second child of Bailey Johnson, Sr. (a Navy dietician) and Vivian (Baxter) Johnson

1931   Maya and her brother, Bailey, Jr. sent to Stamps, Arkansas, to live with their paternal grandmother, Annie ("Momma") Johnson Henderson

1935   Father takes Maya and her brother to St. Louis to live with their mother

1936   Raped by her mother's paramour, Mr. Freeman

1937   Maya and Bailey returned to Stamps, Arkansas

1940	Graduates with honors from Lafayette Country Training School, Stamps; spends time with father in Southern California
1941	Moves to San Francisco to live with her mother and Daddy Clidell
1942	Attends the California Labor School at night
1944	Becomes the first black female trolley car conductor in San Francisco; graduates from Mission High School; her son Clyde (Guy) is born
1949	Marries Tosh Angelos
1952	Marriage to Angelos dissolved
1952	Wins scholarship to study dance with Pearl Primus
1954	First professional performance at the Purple Onion
1954-1955	Tours with the U. S. State Department sponsored company of Gershwin's *Porgy and Bess*
1957	Appears in Off-Broadway Play, *Calypso Heatwave*
1959-1960	Serves as Northern Coordinator, Southern Christian Leadership Conference

1960	Writes, produces, and performs in collaboration with Godfrey Cambridge, "Cabaret for Freedom, " a musical revue; stars in Genet's *The Blacks*
1961	Travels with Vusumzi Make to London and Africa
1961-1962	Associate editor, *Arab Observer* (English-language newsweekly) in Cairo, Egypt; dissolves relationship with Make
1963-1966	Assistant administrator of School of Music and Drama, University of Ghana; works for Ghanian Broadcast Corp. and *Ghanian Times* newspaper, Accra, Ghana; appears in "Mother Courage."
1966	Lecturer, University of California, Los Angeles; acts in Jean Anouilh's *Medea*
1968	Writes and produces a ten-part PBS television series on African traditions in American life—"Black, Blues, Black"
1970	*I Know Why the Caged Bird Sings* (nominated for National Book Award); appointed writer-in-residence, University of Kansas; Yale University Fellowship
1971	*Just Give Me a Cool Drink of Water 'Fore I Diiie* (poetry); Pulitzer Nominee
1972	*Georgia, Georgia* (screenplay)

1973	Marries Paul Du Feu; makes Broadway debut in *Look Away*; nominated for Tony Award for performance
1974	Directs film, *All Day Long*; *Gather Together in My Name*; adapts Sophocles "Ajax"
1975	*Oh Pray My Wings are Gonna Fit Me Well* (poetry); Rockefeller Foundation Fellowship in Italy; honorary degrees from Smith and Mills Colleges; *Ladies' Home Journal* Woman of the Year Award
1976	*Singin' and Swingin' and Gettin' Merry Like Christmas*; honorary degree from Lawrence University; appointed a Bicentennial Commissioner by President Ford
1977	"And Still I Rise" (one-act musical); plays Kunta Kinte's grand-mother in television mini-series, *Roots*; earns Emmy Nomination; National Commission on the Observance of International Women's Year appointment from President Carter
1978	*And Still I Rise* (poetry)
1979	*I Know Why the Caged Bird Sings* (screenplay); "Sister, Sister" (screenplay)
1980	Marriage to Paul Du Feu dissolved; *The Heart of a Woman*

1981 Lifetime appointment as Reynolds Professor of American Studies, Wake Forest University

1983 Honored with Matrix Award given by Women in Communcation, Inc. *Shaker, Why Don't You Sing?* (poetry)

1986 *All God's Children Need Traveling Shoes*

1987 *Now Sheba Sings the Song* (poetry), with sketches by Tom Feelings; North Carolina Award for Literature

1988 Appears on Bill Moyer's PBS program, "The Face of Evil"

1989 *USA Today*'s list of fifty black role models

1990 *I Shall Not Be Moved* (poetry); Candace Award

1993 Presents "On the Pulse of the Morning" at President's Clinton's inauguration; *Wouldn't Take Nothing for my Journey Now* (essays)

1995 David Frost Interview; reads "A Brave and Startling Truth" at 50th Anniversary of United Nations; gives a reading at Million Man March, Washington, D.C.

Chapter 1

Angelou and Autobiography

Maya Angelou creates books that abound in engrossing narratives, dramatic perspectives, and unique similes and metaphors. She is essentially a humorous, affirmative writer whose work is at once centrally feminine and broadly human, meaning the point-of-view is that of a woman with character interactions related to responses observed and understood non-judgmentally. Helen M. Buss suggests that a subjectivity of a divided self is common to a female autobiography such as Angelou's *I Know Why the Caged Bird Sings* by virtue of the literary devices of hyperbole and meiotics. Extensive detail surrounds some anecdotes while diminution of self dominates others.[1] In her narratives Angelou follows the standard underlying plot patterns commonly found in all autobiographies: anticipation, recognition, and fulfillment. At the same time, she adheres to the Aristotelian formula for drama: plot, character, spectacle, and language. Angelou tells in her books wide-ranging, readable stories. Some of these tales are bizarre, some pathetic, some tragic; many are highly amusing, all are exceptionally entertaining. Poetic by nature, Angelou has chosen to intersperse books of poetry with her five autobiographies and a collection of personal essays. A significant linkage of these works is the frequent embracing and reflection of the folklore of her race.

Angelou weaves the biographical facts of her early life in Stamps, Arkansas together with the many anecdotes she tells about her childhood in the first of her autobiographies, *I Know Why the Caged Bird Sings* (1970). Angelou evidences indignation of white supremacy in her writing, but finds balance from within herself and particularly from her sense of humor which shows a strong reliance upon African-American folklore. *Caged Bird* in particular seems dependent on this folklore known as Mother Wit. Wisdom evidenced by Grandmother Henderson throughout the book is obviously the collected wisdom of rural counterparts. The humor found in Stamps is the encompassing humor of African-American survival. This perspective has been influential in the development of my analysis of Angelou's work. In fact, the use of humor in various forms is a strong thread binding together all the works of Angelou. Mary Jane Lupton develops at length a unifying element of motherhood in Angelou's autobiographies. Lupton agrees with Stephen Butterfield that the interplay between mother and child figures creates a continuity. Lupton also indicates a connection between the five volumes based on creative work and motherhood. These references are valid and embraced by several critics who have discussed them at length. However, these penetrating observations lack the subtlety of the comedic connection.[2] This will be analyzed in the next chapter.

Caged Bird takes Angelou from early childhood through high school graduation and the birth of her son. The four subsequent prose books continue her life story, proceeding chronologically. *Gather Together in My Name* (1974) covers her life as a teenage mother, her introduction to drugs and illicit activities, and the travails of basic economic survival. Her young adult years as a show business personality and participation in a *Porgy and Bess* European tour for the U.S. State Department provide the content of book three, *Singin' and Swingin' and Gettin' Merry Like Christmas* (1976). Life as an activist embroiled in social causes is recalled in *The Heart of a Woman* (1981). The final autobiography of the series, *All God's Children Need Traveling Shoes* (1986), explores her experiences as an expatriate in Ghana. The book of essays, *Wouldn't Take Nothing for My Journey Now* (1993), while not a part of the autobiographical sequence, contains material consistent with that genre and provides a forum for philosophizing from the base of Angelou's lifetime experiences.

Angelou has been criticized by reviewer Daisy Aldan for harboring a "fanatic hostility expressed toward all white people."[3] In *Writers at Work* (1958), an interviewer of Robert Penn Warren mentioned a then prevailing literary opinion that "(race problems) have no place in literature," implying that authors should write on universal subjects to achieve literary credibility. Warren responded, "How can you expect a Southern Negro not to write about race, directly, or indirectly, when you can't find a Southern white man who can avoid it."[4] Similarly, other critics such as Frank Lentricchia who contends that "nothing that passes through a human mind doesn't have its origin in sexual, economic, and racial differentiae,"[5] and Elizabeth Fox-Genovese who says, "race and gender lie at the core of any sense of self" agree with Warren.[6] Thus, inasmuch as the African-American Maya Angelou was brought up in the segregated South during the depressed economic conditions of the 1930s, it follows that a substantial amount of her literary work deals with race relations as perceived from

her isolated community's folklore inspired traditions and
lessons. Angelou's observations in these areas are not
always tempered. She recalls the daily degradation visited
upon her people with justifiable acidity. However, daily
chores such as feeding the hogs (*CB* 13-14) are recalled
with gentle humor rather than as harsh memories. Despite
perceived overtones, the thrust of most of Angelou's
writings follows Langston Hughes' expressed literary aim
for his work: "To explain and illuminate the Negro
condition in America."[7] Angelou generally manages to
accomplish this goal in her varied literary efforts without
alienating readers of any race. She does not waste time
whining or determining blame. She accepts what she must
and changes what she can.

Although Angelou has been eminently successful in
several genres, she earned her considerable critical and
personal reputation from the five autobiographies. This
form is considered the oldest and most popular genre in
American literature and the most democratic.[8] However,
according to Angelou, not very many American writers
entrust their entire literary efforts to the autobiographical
form, and she once claimed that no other serious writer
uses autobiography exclusively to convey their work and
expressions.[9]

According to Lynn Z. Bloom, the canon of
autobiography has changed in the past thirty years from a
"single body of work to multiple canons,"[10] and each of
Angelou's five personal narratives embraces the following
canons delineated by Bloom: contemporary
autobiographies; feminist autobiographies; and childhood
autobiographies.

Contemporary autobiographies written by African
Americans are rooted in their historical predecessors. The
personal form of slave narratives and of autobiographies

has been used by African Americans for years to convey their many messages: anger, hope, achievement, vigor, and creativity. This mode records how white hatred and the misery of poverty were confronted. It makes known the positive pervasiveness of caring in segregated communities. Much of African-American folklore derives from these early writings and recorded experiences. Inspiration for an entire race is preserved in this manner. The seeds of perseverance and survival are nurtured.

In validating Angelou's choice of this form and expanding upon its importance, several observations are appropriate. James Olney notes, "Autobiography, straight and fictional, has been the heart and soul of Afro-American literature from the beginning to the present time; no similar claim could be made about the literature of the white South."[11] George E. Kent traces the autobiographical tradition of African Americans from the first major slave narrative of Gustavus Vassa, published in 1789. Kent identifies a main theme in these works as being "A journey through chaos." He credits such writings as having variety, from simple success stories, as exemplified by John Mercer Langston, to the psychological tilt of Katherine Dunham or straight memoirs reported by John Roy Lynch. The confusion of signals and situations visited upon African Americans moved them from hope and belief in the American Dream to Richard Wright's questioning of that dream in *Black Boy*. Wright opened the door for rejection of a status quo, but still held out some hope. Later autobiographers such as Malcolm X and Huey Newton drifted further from previously centrally held ideals and dismissed the remnants of hope in an American dream.[12] Maya Angelou follows many accepted traditions of a "black" autobiographical canon, but begins where a white, Henry Thoreau, suggests every writer should begin:

with a "simple and sincere account of (her) life."[13] Thus in universal terms was born *I Know Why the Caged Bird Sings* and its four succeeding autobiographical volumes, each of which stands alone but is linked to the next.

Despite her traditional incorporations, Kent attributes to Angelou the creation of a unique interpretation for autobiographical form. He cites her presentations for allowing a diversity of expression and a delineation of life in the African-American milieu not previously explored. Her counter-play of the religious and blues traditions is mentioned by several critics in addition to Kent as being an approach worthy of more expansive development. She has found a voice singularly appropriate to black experience. Kent feels this introduction of ethnic culture by Angelou establishes her place in literature. These intrinsic folkloric elements, religion and blues, serve as bridges to a racially aware audience.

The deeply-ingrained religious traditions with its gospel hymns and spirituals learned from daily lessons as a child in Stamps and the specific knowledge of rhythm and blues music acquired from her mother in St. Louis and while clerking at a San Francisco record store and as a performer unconsciously permeate the structure of the writings of Maya Angelou and influence its flow. A cultural identity unavoidably develops from these sources. They are part and parcel of the very being of the Maya character.

Three familiar themes of African-American autobiography and folklore frequent both the prose and poetry of Angelou: repeated triumphs over obstacles, including numerous betrayals; the search for identity, culminating in self-reliance; and the promotion of literacy and learning. Moreover, as James Olney reports, "There is the pattern of bondage, flight and freedom. . .found in virtually all black autobiography,"[14] and which is an integral part of Angelou's work. She adds a universal theme addressing all humans as being more alike than unalike, refusing the hardening of the human spirit.

Angelou writes not just of what has happened to her but its effect upon her. Her books unfold what she has learned, how she has grown, and how she moved along the trail of self-discovery. She lets her stories tell themselves, and from these stories emerge the expositions of a theme. Angelou's dedication to growth and self-evaluation comes up repeatedly: how she modifies, for example, her ideas about black-white relationships. Despite early environmental conditioning, she eventually realizes, as did her friend Malcolm X, that not all whites are devils, thus negating a major obstacle to a free and open life. In other words, her acceptance of disparate points of view marked her growth from an either-or thinker where things are always black or white to looking at events in a gray light. This freedom of thought allowed a break of limiting bondage and the need to seek new arenas depicted in each volume of Angelou's autobiographies. Freedom is found through mental adjustments rather than physical displacements.

The theme of personal identification described in *All God's Children Need Traveling Shoes* reminds Angelou that you can't really leave home. African by definition but American by birth, both influence her being. When Angelou once called herself a "Stampsonian," she admitted a recognition of being firmly planted in traditional Southern culture, and she can't slough off that influence. Her bondage and flight cannot be denied. She accepts that a person is marked by genetic make-up and environmental background, but individual freedom is found internally. She indicated in at least one interview that one's background is ingrained beneath fingernails and hair twists and the song of speech.[15] But this is all part of survival, the acceptance of the individual and self and the realization of the worthiness of all.

An important corollary to freedom and survival is protest, which, Angelou says, "is an inherent part of 'her' work."[16] But she warns that protest should be tempered: serious consideration of protest is required to avoid dangers of interpretation.[17] Angelou avoids using polemics, or lecturing or deliberately structuring her anecdotes to be obvious platforms for advancing social or political ideas, but she lets her stories carry the message. She avoids what Robert Penn Warren in 1958 objected to about the practices of some published writers:

> Protest *qua* protest denies the textures of life. The problem is to permit the fullest range of life into racial awareness. I don't mean to imply that there's nothing to protest about, but aside from the appropriate political, sociological, and journalistic concerns, the problem is to see the protest in its relation to other things. Race isn't an isolated thing--I mean as it exists in the U. S.--it becomes a total symbolism for every kind of issue.[18]

Further maintaining the tradition of what has been labeled black autobiography, Angelou incorporates principles from slave narratives such as recognition of the work-ethic. As Stephen Butterfield observes, "Most of (slave) narratives embrace the work-ethic. . .despite the fact that slaves were stereotyped by whites as lazy and had no reason, given the conditions, to work for their masters any more than was necessary to avoid punishment."[19] Angelou promotes the value of work throughout her autobiographies and as central to some of her poetry. Her basic initial themes of overcoming difficulties and finding self-worth are repeatedly advanced by Angelou as part of a strong work-ethic in her world. Everyone Angelou knew in her community worked hard: her family at the store; the men folk in the fields and mills; and the women in the homes of the whites. In short, "The moral assumptions of the slave narrative," according to Butterfield, "include not only temperance, honesty, worship of God and Christ but also 'respect for hard work.'"[20] Many native folktales incorporate these virtues. These tales counter the stereotypes promoted by racists and are utilized by many African-American writers including Angelou. She dispels negative images whenever possible.

The second of Bloom's autobiographical canons embraced by Angelou is that defined as "feminist." This is seen as a gender based perception of events, the male versus the female outlook. The inclusion of Angelou in Henry Louis Gates, Jr.'s *Reading Black, Reading Feminist* validates her adherence to Bloom's canon. Gates determines that current black women writers found their voices around 1970 and are linked to a 19th century tradition and mind-set. Women's many roles motivate and fill their writing.[21] Keneth Kinnamon suggests that ". . . more than male writers, women are concerned with such themes as community, sexism (especially sexual exploitation), and relations with family and friends."[22] Joanne Braxton agrees and finds such themes to be "traditional in autobiography by black American women. These include the importance of the family and the nurturing and rearing of one's children as well as the quest for self-sufficiency, self-reliance, personal dignity, and self-definition."[23] These abstracts can be found throughout women's literature. While it is true that women "seem correspondingly less interested in individual rebellion, alienation, and success against the odds, as Richard Wright's work seems to suggest,"[24] Angelou's writings do relate one confrontation after another: between a black and

a white; between Angelou and a white housewife; between
Angelou and a white salesgirl; between a white boxer and
a black one; even between Angelou and her white husband.
These confrontations, however, are not presented as
feminist issues, but rather as racial situations. They do not
impact upon a gender interpretation. Their inclusion is to
demonstrate everyday race conflict. It has been noted that
all black autobiography will include a confrontation scene.
Elizabeth Janeway notes in her essay on women's
literature, "That to be distinct from men's literature
women's literature must constitute 'an equally significant
report from another, equally significant, area of
existence.'"[25]   Hence, some of the major themes of
women's literature are "madness, powerlessness, betrayal,
and victimization."[26] These themes can be found frequently
in the works of Angelou. They will be identified as
individual writings are discussed.

Angelou's autobiographies are representative of books
written by African-American women published in the late
sixties and thereafter in which "the writers were more
outspoken about pride in their race than in themselves as
women,"[27] although the authors as women remain the
focus. Several critics writing specifically about Angelou
have found common ground. Selwyn Cudjoe in his study
"Maya Angelou and the Autobiographical Statement" finds:
"the Afro-American autobiographical statement emerges as
a *public* rather than a *private* gesture, *me-ism* gives way to
our-ism and superficial concerns about an individual subject
usually give way to the *collective subjection* of the group."
He adds, "It is never meant to glorify the exploits of the
individual, and the concerns of the collective
predominate."[28] In a similar vein, Joanne Braxton observes
that "unlike the solitary but representative male hero 'who
belts with his fists and his feet,' the black woman

autobiographer uses language--sass, invective, impertinence, and ritual invocation--to defend herself physically and psychologically. As often as not, she celebrates a collective rather than an individual achievement."[29]   G. Thomas Courser proposes that Angelou's autobiographies are "prophetic autobiography, a genre characterized by the conflation of the personal and communal history."[30]   In short, female writers tend to include the universal when writing about the particular. Angelou's body of particulars utilizes all of the above women and ethnic universal characteristics as detailed by the mentioned commentators.

Noting "the verbal wit and clever rejoinders of Miss Jane in *The Autobiography of Miss Jane Pittman* and her readiness to do verbal battle, Barry Beckham points out that ". . .the only way the black Southerner can assert her womanhood short of rebellion may be through the *word*. And often this practice of signifying or verbally abusing another is also necessary to preserve one's humanity against the hostility of other blacks."[31]   But the verbal expertise of women cuts across all races and cultures. Current linguistic research by Deborah Tannen in *You Just Don't Understand* notes that "women are more facile with language than men because being weaker physically, they must hone verbal invective in order to counter the physical strength of men."[32]   Word cleverness is basic to Maya Angelou. She extolls the love of language and admittedly enjoys playing with words. Her words advance her causes and cleverly conquer her adversaries in confrontations. Her readers are treated to lively, original metaphors and phrases.

In all autobiographies, the writer has the power of selecting the material, and therefore the product is subject to self-service or bias. The writer can exercise influence and personal opinion by careful choice of the remembered events presented.   Angelou attempts to balance the remembered events between the pleasant memories such as her relationship with the erudite Mrs. Flowers of Stamps, and the unpleasant ones, the mocking of "momma" by powhitetrash teenagers. She thus enhances the reality and verity of her recollections.   This balance of personal material allows her to validly insert folkloric communal anecdotes.

Childhood is Blooms's third canon of autobiography embraced by Angelou. According to Richard M. Coe in his *When the Grass Was Taller*, which focused exclusively on an examination of autobiographies of childhood, these autobiographies are authored mainly by established writers. Angelou, having acquired credentials as a professional, qualifies to present her autobiography of childhood, *I Know Why the Caged Bird Sings*, under Coe's precept.

One can often look back with fondness or sorrow on childhood, but these times are not usually considered fascinating or worthy of being chronicled.   Coe claims "triviality is the very essence of childhood experience."[33] And William Kinsella said that in his childhood "nothing interesting ever happened to (him)."[34]   William Kennedy quotes Faulkner who said "the problems of children are not worth writing about."[35] These counter comments do not negate the importance of the influences of these years and events in shaping a person nor do they refute that some childhood experiences deserve recall.   The systematic segregation and racism that Angelou endured and observed as a child, and the traumatic rape that she suffered cannot be dismissed lightly or considered inconsequential in her development.   Her judgment of future events is unavoidably colored by the lessons learned and experienced in her tightly-knit segregated society. Her personal guilt regarding swift street justice following her rape weighs heavily upon her young life. To a child, a simple cause and effect results from being "good" or "bad" and is consistent with Lawrence Kohlberg's first stage of moral development.

Coe's study defines this genre, which he calls "the Childhood," as an autobiographical work "*whose structure reflects step by step the development of the writer's self.*"[36] Coe's analysis "applies particularly to sensitive, introspective, often iconoclastic or idealistic writers critical of the segment of society they encounter as children and adolescents."[37] This statement may be appropriate to Angelou. In his chapter, "Portrait of the Artist Surrounded by Family and Friends," Coe identifies some of the common characteristics of childhood:

> In the life of every child there are encountered certain irreducible facts. There is the fact. . .the guilt, indeed the sin-- of having been born. And of having. . .a mother. Perhaps, and putatively, a father. Of being dependent, ineffective, and small. There is the fact of having to rely, complacently or disgustedly, upon the ministrations of others, unchosen and uninvited. . . . Of growing up. Of willy-nilly being educated. Of being Awful. Of discovering the world and one's own body; its prowesses, its demands and its fiascoes. Of falling in love or soaring in lust.[38]

In his study of 600 childhood autobiographies, Coe could have easily included *I Know Why the Caged Bird Sings* because it contains most of his general elements. Angelou is "Awful" because she is a "too-big Negro girl, with nappy black hair, broad feet and a space between her teeth that would hold a number-two pencil. . . ." (*CB* 2) and wears hand-me-down clothes. She had a mother and a father, but the father was never affectionate. She was dependent, ineffective, and small (young). She had to rely on the ministrations of others--her grandmother and family. She discovered the world and her own body alone as an adolescent. At that time, she didn't fall in love or soar in lust, but she did question her sexual identity and seeks determination from a deliberate liaison. She became pregnant from that first encounter and thus was forced to move beyond childhood and its attendant guilts.

Another characteristic of written childhood references, according to Coe, is that "poverty is the significant element in the genre almost from earliest times."[39] Angelou's hometown of Stamps in the 1930s suffered along with the rest of America the severe economic depression. Poverty was everywhere. Although Angelou's grandmother owned a general merchandise store, her household suffered only a degree less than other families. In spite of the difficult conditions, Angelou makes a special point to note that her family did not have to go on relief. This serves to disabuse the reader of the notion that all African Americans existed on federal subsistence. Nonetheless, in *I Know Why the Caged Bird Sings* there is found the "rough correlation between poverty that accompanies so many of our childhoods and the intensity of minute and detailed observation in the refashioning of that childhood experienced by the adult poet."[40] A further observation of Coe's is that autobiographies of childhood usually come from families "with a strong element of emotional imbalance."[41] The rape of the child Angelou introduces a period of great emotional strain. Her imbalance, however, was countered by the strength of her grandmother Henderson who gave to Angelou tough love and a stability. Without formal psychological counseling, Momma found someone to break through the self-imposed silence resulting from the child's response to the rape event.

According to William Kennedy, "It's not that children

in trouble are not great subjects, but what you need is a world and a way of approaching the world. . . . It's the sense of response, as opposed to problem."[42] Angelou responds to the problems of childhood by creating a persona. Encouraged by her literary friends, James Baldwin, John O. Killens, and others to be "bodacious enough to invent her own life daily," she created a fictionalized person who is carried and defined by various narratives. She invented herself because she was tired of society inventing her, of distorting her personality, of turning the stereotype into reality, of carrying a label bestowed on her by outsiders. She found the freedom to express her own feelings and opinions unburdened by the interpretations of others. Stephen Butterfield claims "that the main burden of the black writer. . .has been to repair the damage inflicted on him by white racism, rend the veil of white definitions that misrepresent him to himself and the world, (and) create a new identity."[43] Thus Angelou continues the mission of African-American writers through her structured recollections and reinforces the worth of her people by her recorded accomplishments, both real and invented.

Ernest Gaines says of his early reading of fiction about the South:

> I did not care for the way the black characters were drawn . . . . Whenever a black person was mentioned in these novels, either she was a Mammy or he a Tom; and if he was young, he was a potential Tom, a good nigger; or he was not a potential Tom, a bad nigger. When a black woman character was young, she was either a potential Mammy or a nigger wench. For most of these writers, choosing something between was unheard of.[44]

While Angelou is an autobiographer and not a "fiction"

writer, she purposefully populates her narratives with characters who belie that stereotyped, two dimensional picture of African Americans: Momma; brother Bailey; Vivian Baxter; Daddy Clidell; the two Flowers, Bertha and Martha; Angelou's son; Mr. Elders; Martin Luther King; Malcolm X; Julian Mayfield; all are strong figures. And the persona Angelou created for herself is very close to the real life Angelou: both are articulate, imaginative, witty, strong, independent individuals. She is an intelligent personality rather than the vapid, cheerful know-nothing of a novelist's creation. She deliberately rejects common caricatures.

Angelou concedes having difficulty writing autobiography as literature. She explains that a distance must be established so that the writer is addressing the proper time-frame.[45] When she wrote the teleplay *I Know Why the Caged Bird Sings* she "would refer to the 'Maya' character so as not to mean me (herself). It's damned difficult (for) (me) to preserve this distancing. But it's very necessary."[46] In other words, when Angelou writes about the feelings of a twelve year old, it must reflect the feelings of that age, not the feelings in retrospect.[47] She isolates herself to reach back, free of current influences.

For her actual writing, Angelou reports the first thing she does is to find the rhythm in a subject, the "natural rhythm" of a piece. This rhythm dictates her flow and style within the structure she has chosen. The rhythm Angelou refers to has been recognized as derivative of the native religious and jazz rhythms previously noted. There emerges a comfortable swing of highs, lows, and bridges that envelopes the reader.

Because autobiography is individual revelation, it is falsely assumed that these revelations will be the unvarnished truth. Elizabeth Bruss defines autobiography as "a purportedly true work in which the autobiographer is the source of the subject matter."[48] Richard Coe observes that in autobiography the "border-line between fact and poetry is impossible to determine."[49] It is not surprising to discover that wide-spread distrust exists about absolute truth in autobiography. William Maxwell says, "In talking about the past we lie with every breath we draw."[50] Mark Twain and Woody Allen offer similar realistic comments. Sheldon Kipp rather harshly concludes, "reminiscence is an art that intermingles fact with fiction and unconsciously edits each retelling of our tales. Any personal vignette told exactly the same way more than twice is likely to be a deliberate lie."[51] We have already established the use of fiction by Angelou. A gentler interpretation of Kipp's holds that any story told more than twice qualifies as folklore. Houston A. Baker, Jr. says that folklore is the very basis of black literature. He also points out that written black folklore has a recent history, having been in development only about 300 years. It therefore contains far more contemporary material than the lore of other groups.[52] As previously postulated, Angelou's first autobiography, *I Know Why the Caged Bird Sings*, includes a heavy concentration of amusing and entertaining folk tales and language, much of which is of current derivation. This reflects the material of childhood conditioning. Folklore, however, becomes less obvious in Angelou's succeeding autobiographies as she experiences personal growth. The early influence of folklore has a natural impact upon a child and its strength is no doubt directly related to the isolation and internalization of a particular community.

While folklore permits certain distortions of fact, especially in autobiographical works, writers of pure fiction can be expected to be extremely expedient with the truth.

Their comments range from John Cheever's statement, "I have been a story teller since the beginning of my life, rearranging facts in order to make them more interesting and sometimes more significant,"[53] reasoning "that it is not the facts that we can put our fingers on which concern us but the sum of these facts; it is not the data we want but the essence of the data,"[54] to William Kinsella frankly admitting that "Ninety percent of what I write is just imagination. Imagination is so much more interesting than real life. My life is dull. If I wrote autobiographical stories I wouldn't be making a living as a writer."[55] What these writers strive for is not the pure unvarnished encyclopedic truth but plausibility. A. B. Guthrie tells us "Plausibility is the morality of fiction."[56]

Thus if Angelou needs any justification for varying facts or stretching details, it is easily found. She has license to fictionalize, to enhance interest. Although she admitted creating a persona, she has never admitted to re-defining the facts in her stories. Angelou is attuned to reaching her audience. Her editor once said that she could rewrite a book by completely turning it around and letting the original ending serve as a beginning, using the same facts in a different order for a different impact. In an interview, the real Uncle Willie admitted that "some part of the book (*I Know Why the Caged Bird Sings*) could have been fictional. I wouldn't say it is all true," he said. "I suppose all books have some fiction in them."[57] One can assume that "the essence of the data" is present in Angelou's work. Angelou parallels Kinsella who said, "I found a good voice to tell the stories and I think I understand the way any oppressed group survives is by making fun of the people who oppresses them."[58] It follows that many of the anecdotes Angelou tells have been told before and usually at the expense of the oppressors: whites. These stories have been handed to Angelou via her traditional folklore. Her personal embellishments obscure their roots to the casual reader, thus they appear to be occurrences unique to her and fitted to her literary framework.

Angelou's potential as a writer could be discerned when she was still a child in Stamps. At the age of nine she wrote a descriptive passage about Arkansas quoted by Dr. Dolly McPherson in her dissertation on Angelou and by Esther Hill in an article which showed Angelou's promising facility with words: "Such jolting, rumbling, squeaking and creaking!   Such ringing of cowbells as the cattle plodded along!"[59] This is the same age at which Angelou admits to discovering a love for Shakespeare and learning much from his work.   She credits her reading and memorizing a considerable amount of poetry such as all 1800 lines of Shakespeare's "The Rape of Lucrece" with shaping her writing.   She also had read the Bible twice at an early age, according to her close friend and colleague, Dr. Dolly McPherson, and memorized many passages. Angelou recalls writing songs when she was fifteen and attempting poetry which was admittedly "bad."   But her style has been characterized as poetic and biblical so her early literary encounters were not without obvious influence.

Angelou fits the description of a natural story-teller as outlined by Russell Miller: ". . .able to set the scene quickly and evocatively, describe the action in rich detail, recount credible dialogue and interject humor with an acute sense of timing."[60] These traits reflect a good listener with a rich oral heritage, and Angelou is certainly that.   She recounts hours spent as a child who is seen but not heard.

Angelou has an ear for dialogue no doubt acquired from those listening hours, and does not falsify her characters with inappropriate language.   She does not sanitize the language or culture of a character in order to make him or her more presentable. She strives for credibility. Her grandmother slips into "Black English" on occasion and drops "s's" and omits verbs in some sentences, as appropriate to her vernacular. Angelou's uneducated folk speak with the grammar and the vocabulary of their background; and the informed and knowledgeable like Mrs. Flowers speak in an appropriate general level. The dialogue comfortably fits the characters. It neither demeans nor inflates and sets the scenes accurately for readers. These scenes provide the canvas upon which Angelou paints her word pictures.

The Angelou descriptive style has been called sensuous. This perhaps reflects her show business experience as a performer. She is keenly aware of emotional impact and demonstrates a tremendous bonding with her readers and listeners. Her style carries great emotional appeal. Angelou's public appearances captivate with words and delivery, and her writing follows this pattern of word awareness and tonal inflection. As noted before, there is a musical lilt to her sentences.

Angelou's treatment of love must be examined in any analysis of her work. There needs to be consideration given to the undercurrent of four kinds of love woven throughout her narratives and her poetry. These perspectives are integral to her content.

Many of Angelou's messages arise from spiritual love. In her twenties, Angelou examined Christian Science and inquired about Judaism, but the pull of the charismatic Christian teaching of her early years was always strong. She never rejected Christianity nor formally severed ties with the Christian Methodist Episcopal Church. This was her early anchor, and it was here that her Bible-quoting "Momma" Henderson held a prominent place. Angelou accepted the existence of a higher being and rejected her first husband's atheistic stance. Angelou was adamant about not wanting her son growing up in a "godless" family. She writes how church attendance made her feel cleansed and whole. The existence of God was a given, as was her love of his word. She later found a similar spiritual love amongst her African brothers and sisters. To this day Angelou is actively and unabashedly involved in her religion as she acknowledges publicly. She credits it as being a great source of strength and a linchpin of her philosophy of life.

Angelou also candidly discusses conjugal love. She is proud that she respected and honored the vows of marriage and did not pursue married men. In her marriage to Tosh Angelos, she speaks of physical passion and the general loving relationship they had until they separated. She describes a number of other loving monogamous relationships--emotional and physical--that she had over the years. In one of her poems, she reflects poetically her admiration of a husband. Her poetry includes a number of frank "love poems." She frequently mentions tender responses between couples she knows. She does not confuse love with sex and praises sincere relationships.

Genuine brotherly or familial love, a third type, exemplifies Angelou's love for her brother, Bailey; and for her mother, grandmother, and Uncle Willie, and their love of her. Her grandmother's and mother's love were unconditional, the kind of love she admired in her poem, "The Mothering Blackness." The total, fierce, unquestioning love of Angelou for her son is her ultimate expression of this love. Her love for the writer activist Julian Mayfield was deep and strong, and in no way erotic. Angelou said that a black woman, because of economic and other pressures, needs a brother to tell her when she strays from the accepted norm, and Mayfield fulfilled this need. Her poems about freedom fighters are additional expressions of love and admiration. Her books are filled with characters who exhibit unselfish consideration and love of her and each other.

Finally, there is Eros, sexual love, love without emotional content. Sexual love can exist in marriage as well as can conjugal love, but is generally taken to be outside the marital state. Throughout her books she sprinkles references to purely physical encounters, her own and others. She offers no judgment of these relationships. They are accepted as natural occurrences and are not subject to moralistic preaching. The satisfaction of a human need to feel loved, even briefly, is regarded as very basic to mankind.

The elements of style and content discussed above are in some manner fashioned to impact upon a particular audience envisioned by the writer. This is not to limit any readership, but rather to provide a particular focus and structure. Langston Hughes wrote that "most of his writing from the very beginning has been aimed largely at a Negro reading public."[61] As for Angelou's audience, Stephen H. Butterfield's assumption in *Black Autobiography in America* seems valid: "H. Rap Brown, Donald Reeves, Leslie Lacy, and Maya Angelou all seem to regard the black audience as primary, although they are conscious of whites looking on from the wings."[62] Francoise Lionnet-McCumber's assertion, however, that Angelou's primary audience is "white, urbanized, and educated" because Angelou uses "standard English (rather than dialectal speech patterns)"[63] in *I Know Why the Caged Bird Sings* seems patronizing. She implies that no African American can understand or be comfortable with standard English, a patently false assumption. Obviously the author is comfortable with her competence to write standard English and be understood.

A teller of tales writes to be heard, and Angelou has written portions of her life and black life experiences to be heard by all. The extent of coverage included by Angelou is still undetermined. At a conference on autobiography at Arkansas State University, Josephine Humphreys, a novelist from South Carolina, said "that autobiographies are like a long drive across Arkansas, something done once but not done twice."[64] Contrary to this observation, which elicited the expected laugh, it remains a fact that many writers have produced more than one volume of autobiography. A life journey can have several segments, just as one long drive can consist of many short trips. Originally Angelou's publishers thought of her autobiography as a five-volume series. They may well be right. In 1976 she commented upon the volumes of autobiography contemplated at that time. She anticipated a run of seven or eight books if both she and her interest survived long enough.[65] Her interest appears to have diminished although in 1987, she mentioned planning one more volume of autobiography, extending the series up to the time of publication of *I Know Why the Caged Bird Sings* and no further. She considers this as a cut-off that would preclude writing about the mechanics of writing, which would not interest her.[66] Her plate has been full in recent years, and while we may not see more of her life-stories, her voice will be heard in one form or another. She still has things to say. Her recent collection of essays, *Wouldn't Take Nothing for My Journey Now*, proves this point. Angelou is an active observer and commentator on current trends and fits comfortably in the *griot's* chair.

Notes

[1]Helen M. Buss, "Reading for the Doubled Discourse of American Women's Autobiography," *Auto/Biography Studies*, 5, 1 (1991) 95-98.

[2]Mary Jane Lupton, "Singing the Black Mother: Maya Angelou and Autobiographical Continuity," *Black American Literature Forum*, 24, 2 (Summer 1990), 257-276.

[3]Daisy Aldan, Review of "*The Heart of a Woman*," *World Literature Today* 56, 4 (1982): 697.

[4]Malcolm Cowley, ed., *Writers at Work* (New York: Viking, 1958) 203.

[5]Quoted in "A Constellation of Recently Hired Professors Illuminate the English Department at Duke," *Chronicle of Higher Education* 27 May 1987: 13.

[6]Elizabeth Fox-Genovese, "Between Individualism and Fragmentation. . .," *American Quarterly* 42, 1 (1990): 28.

[7]Quoted in James A. Emanuel, *Langston Hughes* (New York: Twayne, 1967) 68.

[8]Frances Smith Foster, "Adding Color and Contour to Early American Self-Portraiture," *Conjuring*, ed. Marjorie Pryse and Hortense Spillers (Bloomington: Indiana University Press, 1985) 26.

[9]Jeffrey M. Elliot, *Conversations with Maya Angelou* (Jackson, MS: University Press of Mississippi, 1989) 39, 195.

[10]Lynn Z. Bloom, Abstract of paper delivered at Modern Language Association Convention, December 1990, no page number.

[11]James Olney, "Autobiographical Traditions, Black and White." *Located Lives*, ed. Bill Berry (Athens: The University of Georgia Press, 1990) 74.

[12]George E. Kent, "Maya Angelou's *I Know Why the Caged Bird Sings* and Black Autobiographical Tradition," 7, 3 *Kansas Quarterly* (1974): 72-78.

[13]Quoted in Lynn Z. Bloom, "Review, Life Studies: Interpreting Autobiography," *College English* 49, 3 (1987): 347.

[14]Olney 77.

[15]Elliot 158.

[16]Elliot 153.

[17]Elliot 159.

[18]Quoted in Malcolm Cowley, *Writers at Work*, 203-204.

[19]Stephen Butterfield, *Black Autobiography in America* (Amherst:

University of Massachusetts Press, 1974) 13.

[20]Butterfield 17.

[21]Henry Louis Gates, Jr., ed. *Reading Black, Reading Feminist* (New York: Meridian, 1990).

[22]Keneth Kinnamon, "Call and Response," *Belief vs. Theory in Black American Literary Criticism*, ed. Joe E. Weixlmann and Chester J. Fontenot (Greenwood, FL: Penkeville, 1986) 133.

[23]Joanne M. Braxton, *Black Women Writing Autobiography* (Philadelphia: Temple University Press, 1989) 184.

[24]Kinnamon 133.

[25]Quoted in E. Miller Budick, "The Feminist Discourse of Sylvia Plath's *The Bell Jar*," *College English* 49, 8 (1987): 872.

[26]Quoted in Budick 872.

[27]Estelle Jelinek, *Women's Autobiography* (Bloomington: Indiana University Press, 1980) 149.

[28]Selwyn Cudjoe, "Maya Angelou and the Autobiographical Statement," *Black Women Writers*. ed. Mari Evans. (New York: Anchor Books/Doubleday, 1984) 10.

[29]Braxton 205-206.

[30]Quoted in Michael Johnson, "Mary Boykin Chestnut's Autobiography and Biography," *The Journal of Southern History* LXVII, 4 (1981): 591.

[31]Barry Beckham, "Miss Jane and Oral Tradition," *Callaloo* 1,3 (1978): 106.

[32]Deborah Tannen, *You Just Don't Understand* (New York: Morrow, 1980).

[33]Richard M. Coe, *When the Grass Was Taller* (New Haven, Yale University Press, 1984) xii.

[34]William Simonsen, "Of Love Stories and Baseball--An Interview with W. P. Kinsella," *Writers' N.W.* (Summer 1990): 2.

[35]William Kennedy, "The Art of Fiction," *The Paris Review* 112 (Winter 1989): 55-56.

[36]Coe 9.

[37]Bloom, "Review,": 347.

[38]Coe 139.

[39]Coe 206.

[40]Coe 206

[41]Coe 140.

[42]Kennedy 55-56.

[43]Butterfield 6.

[44]Ernest J. Gaines, "Miss Jane and I," *Callaloo* 1, 3 (1978): 26.

[45]Elliot 195.

[46]Elliot 148.

[47]Elliot 106.

[48]Bloom, abstract, no page number.

[49]Coe.

[50]Bloom, "Review,": 345.

[51]Sheldon Kipp, *Who Am I Really* (Los Angeles: Tarcher, 1987), viii.

[52]Houston A. Baker, Jr., *Long Black Song* (Charlottesville: The University Press of Virginia, 1972) 18.

[53]John Cheever, "Journals from the Sixties," *The New Yorker* 21 Jan. 1991: 36.

[54]Cheever 40.

[55]Quoted in Simonsen 2.

[56]A. B. Guthrie, "Novelist Tries to Show Truth," *Jonesboro Sun* 4 Mar. 1991: A2.

[57]Quoted in Jimmy Jones, "Author's Memory of Stamps: Total Segregation," *Arkansas Gazette* 19 July 1970: B 2.

[58]Quoted in Simonsen 2.

[59]Elliot 111.

[60]Russell Miller, *Bare-Faced Messiah* (New York: Holt, 1987) 67.

[61]Quoted in Emanuel 68.

[62]Butterfield 185.

[63]Francoise Lionnet-McCumber, "Autobiographical Tongues: (Self-) Reading and (Self-) Writing in Augustine, Nietzche, Marie Cardinal, Maya Angelou, and Marie-Therese." Dissertation, U of Michigan, 1986, 110.

[64]Josephine Humphreys, "Autobiography as Seduction," a Reading at Arkansas State University, April 1988.

[65]Elliot 49.

[66]Elliot 181.

Chapter 2

Wit and Wisdom/Mirth and Mischief

The high spots of Maya Angelou's childhood years in Stamps, Arkansas in the 1930s were "usually negative: droughts, floods, lynchings and death."[1] To contrast the psychological and physically devastating forces encountered there, she lavishly imbues her prose and poetry with humor. Her philosophy is that every chance one gets, one should laugh. It is interesting to note, however, that in spite of sister support in her writings, Angelou does not align herself with modern feminists because she thinks they do not have a sense of humor. While Angelou's comedy is often born out of pain and anger, she is, nevertheless, secure enough to laugh at herself and with her people. She intentionally incorporates incidents that show her marginally existing community had moments of fun and laughter and a significance as an entity. Twenty odd years ago, Isaac Asimov noted that women rarely took part in joke sessions, and if they did they were almost always passive. Telling a joke is aggressive.[2] Angelou has never been passive in her writings and in her personal life, but neither has she been overtly aggressive. She does not attack indiscriminately just to get a laugh. Her humor is brave and hearty, and while it does have an edge, it is a

humor that is not mean-spirited nor malicious.   For
example, she exempts from her humor some traditional
targets of ridicule: the stuttering of her brother Bailey; and
the physical handicap of her Uncle Willie. Angelou shows
compassion and allows for dignity to those targeted by her
humor.

Little of the anecdotal humor that is found in Angelou's
writings is original with her, although she does evidence
her own strong humorous interpretations and outlook.   In
All God's Children Need Traveling Shoes, Angelou says she
collects jokes.   This may have been an off-hand remark,
but she does exhibit familiarity with much known humor.
Folklore provides a major source of humor, which reflects
Angelou's traditional culture.   This is the humor that
carries *Caged Bird* and is probably more aggressive than
comedy developed outside Mother Wit.

Angelou's mentor in Stamps, a community intellectual,
Mrs. Flowers, encouraged her "to listen carefully to what
country people called Mother Wit," (*CB* 83) which is, Alan
Dundes explains,   ". . . a popular term in black speech
referring to common sense" and "With its connotations of
collective wisdom acquired by the experience of living and
generations past is often expressed in folklore."[3] Everyday
interchanges amongst people of like groupings are replete
with fragments of folklore ranging from involved folk tales
and superstitions to familiar homilies and phrases.
Proverbs or maxims are rules to live by handed down
through the generations. And Angelou's heritage is full of
such instruction.

The definition of folklore is always in a state of flux.
Today's folklorists hold that "the hallmark of folklore is
change, and that for anything to be considered an item of
folklore it must exist in more than one form."[4]   Jan H.
Brunvand states folklore is "those materials in a culture that

circulate traditionally among members of any group in different versions."[5] Daryl Dance in *Shuckin' and Jivin'* reports that "many of the accounts of individual experiences turn out to be in effect folktales."[6] While most if not all folklore is based on actual experiences, the stories do indeed circulate in various forms in a community. Angelou incorporates many stories of personal confrontations that can be corroborated by reference to collections or critical essays on folklore, an example of which is her encounter with Mrs. Cullinan. These chameleon anecdotes meet the test of folklore as defined by the above quotes.

It has been previously noted that Angelou is a natural story teller in the tradition of the African *griot* made familiar in Alex Haley's *Roots*. She is what African-American performers generically call "a man of words." Writing about what she knows, namely the black experience, Angelou approaches her work in the manner of any serious writer. She sometimes describes, sometimes narrates, but most often dramatizes; and overlays her "fiction" with "gravey," to use a preacher term. African-American preachers were expected to provide not only substance to their sermons but also "gravey," emotional content. Folklore humor is the "gravey" of Angelou's narratives.

In *Ethnic Humor Around the World* Christie Davies notes that "it is possible to use jokes to further other purposes . . . ."[7] Isaac Asimov observes that "jokes offer a way of supplying serious commentary in a matter. Abraham Lincoln used jokes in this fashion constantly, and it is possible to argue that Jesus allowed his parables to perform a similar function. . . most dedicated jokesters recognize their hobby. . . as a kind of social commentary. . . ."[8]

Angelou does indeed use jokes and anecdotes "as a kind of social commentary." Her extensive use of humor pointedly demonstrates the dependence of segregated communities on humor and hilarity -- and even on singing; and the existence of such light-heartedness does much to destroy the false assumption that the oppressed are without humor. This is not to imply that an individual was satisfied with his bleak economic, social, and political condition. Frederick Douglass in his *Autobiography* said he "was utterly astonished to find persons who speak of the singing among slaves as evidence of their contentment and happiness. It is impossible to conceive of a greater mistake. Slaves sing most when they are most unhappy."[9] One active jazz composer proclaimed blues music to be optimism in the face of adversity. Joseph Boskin and Joseph Dorinson concur by noting slaves laughed "to keep down trouble and to keep their hearts from being broken;"[10] John Little claims, "I have cut capers in chains."[11] Given their second-class status and the unpredictable behavior of some whites, minorities in the 1930s prudently exercised caution and repressed their resentment. Hiding true feelings was an accepted fact of life. A warning by Angelou's mother, Vivian Baxter, is typical and appropriate. She said, "Never let whites know what you really think. If you're sad, laugh. If you're bleeding inside, dance."[12] Angelou's grandmother, Momma Henderson, didn't "cotton to the idea that white-folks could be talked to at all without risking one's life" (*CB* 39). Thus the inclination to hide behind humor was taught as a natural protective measure.

As a story teller, Angelou is neither abrupt nor curt. She takes short and simple stories and embellishes them fully with her "gravey." In *Caged Bird*, for example, with additions and stretches, she tells fairly lengthy tales about preachers and ghosts. The inclusion of familiar anecdotes (folklore) with herself and her people as central figures serves to demonstrate that a serious event in her community, even a religious service, was not without some lighter moments. Pertinent to this, Isaac Asimov observes that "one of the functions of the joke is to speak the unspeakable. A religion that is never anything but solemn becomes most certainly never anything but mechanical."[13] And the importance of religion in African-American lives reflects its vitality and life-long influence.

The religious practices of Angelou's community in Stamps were often anything but solemn. For example, the "hot" and hilarious religious service that Angelou relates in *Caged Bird* has elements of pure slapstick, and thereby expresses the "unspeakable" in a sacred setting. During this service a Sister Monroe, emotionally overwhelmed by the sermon, approaches the Reverend Thomas and in her enthusiasm hits him on the back of his head with her purse so hard that his false teeth "jumped out of his mouth" (*CB* 35). Richard Dorson's *Negro Folktales in Michigan* contains a similar story of a Mississippi preacher whose false teeth jumped out of his mouth during a sermon.[14] This anecdote is often repeated in various settings, and while attributable to the extreme emotional impact of serious religious fervor, it serves to lighten the service for less responsive parishioners and still keep them attentive.

An earlier bit of folklore in *Caged Bird* concerns a scuffle in the church described as a fall-down slapstick comedy scene which elicits Angelou's reaction that "There wasn't time to laugh or cry before all three of them were down on the floor behind the altar" (*CB* 33). Angelou did laugh at the happenings and was properly whipped for her involuntary, inappropriate response. The sincere emotional reactions in a religious setting were not to be diminished by snickers. However, for weeks after, she reports that she "stood on laughter's cliff and any funny thing could hurl (her) off to her death far below" (*CB* 37). This fear of falling is often experienced by children, but Angelou uses it in an imaginative, striking, and amusing metaphor. She combines the folklore of the raucous church event with a personalized, original conclusion. At the same time, she acknowledges that disrespect is punishable.

Angelou presents a familiar and believable mix of tradition and innovation. Many standard preacher stories "pit the poor against those in power," as Daryl Dance observes,[15] and the Negro preachers have become symbolic of the mundane flaws of authority figures. Food, sex, money, and love were the four things preachers were most interested in, according to the folk stories. These interests are also traditional male concerns. At that time, the preachers were male, and because eight-five percent of the members of the flock were women, the preacher was, as one critic expressed it, "a rooster in charge of the hen house."[16] As an authority figure complete with jousting followers, the preacher was obviously a ready target for ridicule, a butt for jokes.[17]

Such a figure is Angelou's Reverend Thomas, the presiding church elder from Texarkana who visits the church in Stamps every three months. He is hated "unreservedly" by both Angelou and her brother. They considered the Reverend to be "ugly and fat,"[18] and "he laughed like a hog with the colic" (*CB* 27). He couldn't even remember their names. Bailey often had fun imitating him, following the tendency of the young to mock authority figures.

Visiting story-preachers always seemed to be eating chicken. In the 1930s, a congregation often couldn't pay a preacher, so they compensated him with elaborate meals, generally featuring chicken. This was considered their "company food," since economics excluded serving anything as expensive as beef. Members of the congregation vied with one another to provide the best meals, and a preacher's popularity could be measured by his girth. A complaint often voiced regarding preachers was their eating "the biggest, brownest and best part of the chicken at every Sunday meal" (*CB* 28). The preacher, of course, felt he was doing justice to the offerings, but "Sunday Best" going to preachers made them open to ridicule and a bit of resentment from those affected by family holdback. Courtesy and hospitality did not always compensate for sacrifice.

Religious folklore dictates an annual gathering and such were the ecumenical revivals held in Stamps. Angelou reports on and contrasts warmly, gently and amusingly the participants in this event. All three Methodist denominations, the "hoity-toity" Mount Zion Baptist Church and even the Church of God in Christ (the Holy Rollers) attended. Angelou recalls the game-like characteristics of the liturgy of these revival meetings, designed to be enjoyed by both adults and children. The gatherings and their patterned liturgies reinforced communal bonds despite denominational differences. Much humor was squirreled away to be secretly laughed over until the next year. (The folklore of such religious gatherings is discussed by William Clements in *A Handbook of Folklore*, published by Indiana University Press.)

Ghost stories also provide a measure of humor in African-American folklore. These stories were traditionally a part of native re-collections. The mandatory ghost story Angelou tells in *Caged Bird* is laced with an odd mingling of humor and fear, as in ghost story motion

pictures; and the objects of the story are Angelou herself
and her neighbors. It would have been abnormal, Angelou
admits, had she not been superstitious. It was quite natural
for her to believe in "hants and ghosts and 'thangs'"(*CB*
140). The ghost story Angelou retells is related in *Caged
Bird* by a George Taylor (not the Reverend), who recently
lost his wife of many years and since then has been taking
his meals with various families around town, and thus he
finds his way to Angelou's family table.

Since any ghost story is meant to frighten, Angelou
establishes the appropriate setting: the wind "whistled
sharp under the closed door," (*CB* 128) and the light in the
room in which they were sitting had an "eerie, harsh
perspective" (*CB* 131). On this particular night, Angelou is
reading *Jane Eyre*, a haunting love story; her brother is
absorbed in *Huckleberry Finn*, an adventure story appealing
to young males; and Uncle Willie, the practical one, is
busy with the *Almanac*. This quiet evening of reading is
interrupted by a knock on the door. It is George Taylor.
Momma invites George to stay for supper, even if they
have to". . . stick some sweet potatoes in the ashes of the
stove to stretch the evening meal" (*CB* 129), as dictated by
normal hospitality. It behooves a guest to "sing for his
supper" and entertain his hosts so George Taylor begins
telling a tale about his dream of the previous night. He
tells of seeing a white baby angel, fat, with blue eyes, and
laughing. In the background, he hears a voice that he
identifies as that of his departed wife, Florida, who is
saying, "I want some children" (*CB* 132). There are at least
two elements of folklore here. Florida's voice coming
from beyond the grave employs the standard device of "a
spirit of the already dead that returns with a definite
purpose."[19] And when Taylor repeats Florida's words, he
follows the speech practices of story tellers by pitching his

"already high voice to what he considered a feminine level" (*CB* 133). These are universally identified devices used to enthrall the listener.

George Taylor's story and his wife, Florida, provide an opportunity for Angelou to poke fun at her own fears. When she describes the funeral service for Florida, she remembers how Florida's quaint voice -- a high pitched one -- could part "the air in the Store" (*CB* 137). And the trip to the cemetery for Florida's burial service occasions Angelou's fear that the thought of the voice of Florida "coming out of the grave . . . was enough to straighten my hair" (*CB* 138). The little child is so gripped with fear by the story Brother Taylor tells about the dead Florida that she "almost tripped onto the stove," a moment of humor which elicits from Momma the cliché: "That child would stumble over a pattern in a rug" (*CB* 139). This serves to soften the frightful specter of Florida's spirit speaking out. With this involved story, Angelou discharges her obligation to include tales of the supernatural. She remains faithful to traditional structure.

Angelou injects throughout her autobiographies comedic incidents that personally befall her but contain subtle elements of universal folklore. She tells of a transient and amusing romance when she was in Ghana with a man who boasts about having become a man at a young age. He passionately pursues Angelou despite his having a wife and several children. This over-amorous, bragging male appears frequently in folklore and is not to be taken seriously. A story in *Gather Together* concerns turning the tables on two California "lesbians," Beatrice and Johnnie May, which demonstrates the folklore victory of a good, naive heroine over the evil know-it-all. A standard Br'er Rabbit story appears in *The Heart of a Woman* to relay the same general message. Br'er Rabbit stories are well known to African-American children.

Stock jokes well-known and often repeated in various cultures are interwoven by Angelou. One such is the teasing joke that brother Bailey tells about the "uglies." This purports to show that the young Bailey has a sense of humor and a harmless mischievous streak -- just like anyone his age:

> "Oh Miseriz (sic) Coleman, how is your son? I saw him the other day, and he looked sick enough to die."
> Aghast, the ladies would ask, "Die? From what? He ain't sick."
> And in a voice oilier than the one before, he'd answer with a straight face, "From the Uglies." (*CB* 17).

Another joke that Angelou tells has a fairly long history in the folklore of the black community. It alleges the prohibition of vanilla ice cream for blacks except on July Fourth, Independence Day. On other days they had to be satisfied with chocolate. (*CB* 40) Angelou's purpose is to show that her community could ridicule the absurdity of racism, thus softening its psychological impact. Langston Hughes in his "Jokes Negroes Tell on Themselves" recalls several restrictions on the word white in the South:

> They say, for example, (presumable in fun) that the reason Negroes eat so many black-eyed peas in Dixie, and in Louisiana so many red beans, it is because for years after the Emancipation, colored people did not dare ask a storekeeper for white beans. Red beans, or black-eyes, okay. But it was not until folks began using the term navy beans, that Negroes had the nerve to purchase white beans, too.[20]

Angelou frequently employs the folkloric devices of boasting and exaggeration. Angelou's description in *Caged*

Bird of the scene at Momma's store, where the workers congregated just before leaving for the cotton fields emphasizes good-natured humor. She writes, ". . . the Store was full of laughing, joking, boasting and bragging. One man was going to pick two hundred pounds of cotton, and another three hundred. Even the children were promising to bring home fo' bits and six bits" (*CB* 6). Another worker claimed, "I'm gonna work so fast today I'm going make you look like you standing still" (*CB* 6) Although Angelou amusingly captures the workers' interplay, her real intention is to show that the work ethic was still strong as pointedly mentioned in the old slave narratives. The syntax is not sanitized and the use of the workers' colloquial diction and verb omission provide the flavor of the joshing. This is a softer humor, a sympathetic teasing.

Rampant exaggeration is often used by brother Bailey in order to spin tall tales or Whoppers, "say about giant vegetables"[21] or the biggest fish. When Bailey returns to Stamps after a visit to St. Louis, he reports, "the cotton up North was so tall, if ordinary people tried to pick it they'd have to get on ladders, so that cotton farmers had their cotton picked by machines" (*CB* 76). Bailey further claimed, "They've got watermelons twice the size of a cow's head and sweeter than syrup" (*CB* 75). He also says that ". . . in the North buildings are so high . . . that for months in winter, you can't see the top floors" (*CB* 75). Such statements represent "the American love of preposterous and ludicrous exaggeration which was at the core of so much early American humor," as Christie Davies notes.[22] Davy Crockett, Pecos Bill and Paul Bunyan tales exemplify this vein.

Angelou has frequently expressed dismay at society's arbitrarily inventing what a person should be -- that is, the tendency to stereotype or perpetuate folklore images. So when the subjects of her humor are whites, she takes the opportunity not only to be funny, but also to disabuse readers of misconceptions and myths about her own race. With these stories, she can demonstrate the absurdity of racism by the process of boomeranging, which is reversing the stereotyped assumption with a sudden sharp alteration in point-of-view. For example, Angelou has commented that when whites say people of color only want sex while whites want love and romance, those making such statements show their ignorance by their acceptance of the ridiculous. Another folk story, no doubt frequently repeated but personalized by Angelou, tells of her Uncle Willie being forced to hide from marauding "Klansmen" in a most unlikely and undignified place -- in a barrel of potatoes and onions. This tale evokes mixed feelings. There is first a disgust that the white sheriff whose duty it was to uphold the law for everyone could warn but not protect Willie from lawless whites; but there is a second response of delight because he emerges physically unscathed and has outsmarted the Klansmen. Thus Willie was the real winner, an important psychological victory for the people, and Momma has fulfilled her maternal role as protector.

Caged Bird contains many examples of irony to jab at racism. One such occurrence is during the Joe Louis and Primo Carnera fight in the 1930s. Angelou recalls the gathering in her grandmother's store to hear on the radio the championship fight. Louis and Carnera represented a concrete black-white conflict. Most professional fighters when tired or dazed often will hold their opponent. This Carnera did to Louis, eliciting the comment, "That white man don't mind huggin' that niggah now, I betcha," (*CB* 112). It was almost sacrilegious for blacks and whites to embrace.[23] Southern whites would never initiate such a gesture. Carnera did not respond to the bell for a round, and those in Momma's store celebrated the Louis victory and cautiously headed for their homes. This anecdote clearly demonstrates the sad irony that even though a black has proven to be the strongest man in the world, they were still vulnerable, and must take care being abroad at night for fear of what a "crazy cracker" might do to them.

Signifying, saying one thing and meaning another, is a favorite device of ethnic groups. This use of indirection to avoid denial or lying, has become embedded in black folk culture to exclude whites or to talk around them. Thus, "If you ask a Negro where he's been, he'll tell you where he is going" (CB 164). Angelou assails those who assume that others are inferior and therefore not people by jokingly noting alleged unfavorable characteristics: "Whitefolks couldn't be people because their feet were too small, their skin too white and see-throughy and they didn't walk on the balls of their feet the way people did -- they walked on their heels like horses" (CB 21). In her second autobiography, Gather Together in My Name, she reverses -- boomerangs -- the frequently expressed white myth that all blacks looked alike and that they all stuck together: "Literally all white folks still looked alike to me: pale and similar" (GT 94); "Whitefolks were so strange. Everybody knew they stuck together better than Negroes did" (CB 90). This quote is immediately recognized by African Americans as an indirection.

A tradition bound "Red Leg" tale is told by Angelou in Caged Bird. It concerns a black confidence man selling some real estate he does not own to a white mark. This "cracker" had bilked so many Negroes that he needs to be victimized, out-witted and tricked by an even sharper black. As a result, poetic justice is rendered to the

"villain." These stories have enjoyed popularity amongst
the down-trodden throughout history. Angelou's Red Leg
tale is a variation on the trickster story of revenge. This is
classified as the Comedy of Revenge and illustrates a major
purpose of humor: namely, that it "is founded on the
deathless principle of seeing someone get the worst of it,"[24]
as James L. Ford writes. Red Leg avenges the
disadvantaged, and Angelou's perspective parallels W. P.
Kinsella's observation, noted above, "I think I understand
the way any oppressed group survives is by making fun of
the people who oppresses them."

A symbolic dramatization of the triumph of the
downtrodden over the supposed elite is Angelou's
rendition of her experience with a white Stamps housewife,
Mrs. Cullinan. There is the wry observation that this
woman's husband probably fathered two children with a
black woman and refused to acknowledge them. This
echoes Frederick Douglass's relating the hypocritical
practice of whites fathering children with their black female
slaves and subsequently rejecting these offspring. It is a
fact that such events occurred in the antebellum South, but
it is not a verifiable fact that Mr. Cullinan bore such guilt.
Angelou is fantasizing, as she does with her mention of a
rumor that his wife is unable to bear children. The textual
inclusion of common gossip emphasizes the outrageousness
and repugnancy of such an arrogant sexual practice. The
lack of ethics thus demonstrated by slave holders indicates
an inherent immorality on their part.

Angelou expands upon her term of subservience to
include a further minor triumph. Angelou was ten when
Mrs. Cullinan's kitchen became her "finishing school." At
first she feels pity for the unattractive woman. But when
the lady repeatedly carelessly and possibly deliberately calls
Angelou Mary, instead of Marguerite, her real name,

Angelou reacts angrily, not because she is "touchy," but because "some white woman could rename her for her convenience" (*CB* 92). The genesis of this resentment goes back to the beginning of slavery, when slaves often had no names or were given them whimsically by slave masters. As the ownership of the slave changed, the name of the slave often changed. This demeaning practice was naturally abhorrent. Every person Angelou knew "had a hellish horror of being 'called out of his name'" (*CB* 91). In retaliation for her employer's thoughtlessness, Angelou "accidentally" breaks a piece of prized china. The youngster thus finds an accepted way to even a score and retain her pride. That "breaking china was probably a common occurrence by black maids,"[25] according to Langston Hughes, gives the anecdote a verisimilitude and a comic tone, minimizing negative behavior.

Angelou brightens her drama with deadpan humor and often ends paragraphs with one-liners, punch lines or zingers. This practice is exemplified by the last sentence of a paragraph describing Mrs. Cullinan:

> On our way home one evening, Miss Glory told me that Mrs. Cullinan couldn't have children. She said that she was too delicate-boned. It was hard to imagine bones at all under those layers of fat. Miss Glory went on to say that the doctor had taken out all her lady organs. I reasoned that a pig's organs included lungs, heart and liver, so if Mrs. Cullinan was walking around without those essentials, it explained why she drank alcohol out of unmarked bottles. *She was keeping herself embalmed.* (Italics added.) (*CB* 89)

Another one-liner paragraph ending is the last line in Angelou's report of Momma's insistence on cleanliness, which also counters a negative perception regarding personal habits:

> Each night in the bitterest winter we were forced to wash faces, arms, necks, legs and feet before going to bed. She used to add, with a smirk that unprofane people can't control when venturing into profanity, "*and wash as far as possible, then wash possible.*" (Italics added.) (*CB* 21)

Exaggeration and overstatement, discussed previously, are devices often used in literature to carry an emotional truth rather than a factual one. This is employed by Angelou in her recorded encounter with a local dentist, Dr. Lincoln, for emergency dental treatment. True, this event might have actually been experienced by Angelou. But the name of the dentist, his language, the fantasy about Momma, and the theme all suggest elements of a folktale, embellished by many retellings. As there is no record of a real Dr. Lincoln practicing dentistry in Stamps in the 1930s, the name is probably a metaphor. The familiar name of Lincoln, the Father of Freedom for slaves, frequently appears in early black literature. Angelou's usage underscores the irony of continued bondage. In the 1930s, dental treatment in the South for African Americans was indeed second-class. They had to enter a professional office from the back. When Angelou and her grandmother visited Dr. Lincoln, they used the back stairs, as expected. Despite this adherence to convention, Dr. Lincoln refused to tend to the girl. He claimed it was against his policy to treat blacks. In an insulting and unoriginal expression the dentist indicated he would". . . rather stick his hand in a dog's mouth than in a nigger's" (*CB* 160). This quote has appeared in other black collections of folklore and is indicative of the crude mores of the general society of that time.

The incident triggers a flight of fantasy and Angelou imagines her grandmother confronting Dr. Lincoln alone and ordering him to leave Stamps by sundown. Momma demands that he pay interest on money he had borrowed from her to save his building, and in a name-calling tour deforce -- a playing-the-dozens routine -- the scenario has her telling him ". . . he'll never again practice dentistry . . ." and that in his next place he "will be a vegetarian caring for dogs with the mange, cats with cholera and cows with the epizootic" (*CB* 162). Dr. Lincoln capitulates and gives Momma ten dollars interest money, acknowledging an indebtedness to her. The dream sequence continues as they leave the office and Momma waves her handkerchief at the nurse and turns her". . . into a crocus sack of chicken feed" (*CB* 162). To the delight of Angelou and her sympathetic readers, Momma "had obliterated the evil white man," (*CB* 162) and the theme of a black getting the better of a white in a one-on-one confrontation is shown once more. This is a make-believe tale based on situational reality and as such is rooted in cultural folklore.

Angelou also takes the opportunity in *Caged Bird* to counter jokes denigrating black soldiers by telling an embellished version of what is called the "lost-arm joke." This joke, which was widely circulated, has crossed all cultures and probably has a European origin. Since Angelou's story encompasses a wartime period -- the early 1940s -- this anecdote is a natural inclusion.

The tale involves an alleged conversation in the early 1940s between a Negro man and a white woman, an unusual occurrence because black men and white women not known to each other rarely conversed. Angelou's version tells about a San Francisco matron during World War II who refuses to sit beside a Negro civilian on a bus. In addition, she chides him for being a draft dodger. She

says that ". . . the least he could do was fight for his
country the way her son was fighting on Iwo Jima" (*CB*
181). The man then moved his arm away from the window,
showing an armless sleeve, and said quietly, "'Then ask
your son to look around for my arm, which I left over
there'"(*CB* 181). In this devastating status interplay,
typically found in television sit-coms where one character
humbles another, the matron's status is lowered and the
man's raised. This is categorized as a race-conscious joke
and is an example of "the retort discourteous" -- the wit of
retaliation -- that serves as a mechanism in the racial
conflicts in America.[26]

This story has cropped up many times in various
settings. John Burma has the matron stating that she has
two sons overseas, as follows:

> A white woman enters a street car; a white soldier
> surrenders his seat which is next to a Negro civilian. She
> says, "I won't sit next to that 4F nigger."
>   The Negro calmly asks, "Have you a son in the
> service?"
>   "I have two, both overseas."
>   "Good," says the Negro, "tell them to look for the right
> arm I left over there."
>   The lady got off the bus at the next stop.[27]

Angelou specifies Iwo Jima in her story because of the
positive connotations of that military event, and thereby
provides the story an even greater impact. The original
story probably had a core of truth in it -- an encounter no
doubt took place between a woman or man and a disabled
soldier sometime in Europe or America. Angelou possibly
heard the story during World War II and repeated it to
enhance pride of race by showing a black soldier
sacrificing with dignity and equality in the fight for

democracy.

As noted previously, Angelou faithfully records the language of people around Momma's store and she purposely rejects cleaning up the diction and grammar of others in her narratives. To accurately capture personality, she weaves in profanity, when it is appropriate to do so. Profanity, in fact, is fairly extensive in all her narratives, reflecting reality. The inclusion of a fair amount of scatological humor that she heard in Stamps has a historic relationship to the language recollections of other African-American writers. It is included not for shock effect purposes but to capture the personalities of the speakers. Regarding Mrs. Cullinan, the young Marguerite says, "I wouldn't pee on her if her heart was on fire" (*CB* 90). She calls Dr. Lincoln, the archetypal dentist in Stamps, a "peckerwood" (*CB* 163). Common descriptive terms are a "giant's fart" (*CB* 100) and "shit color"(*CB* 17). When Angelou blatantly asks a young man in San Francisco if he"would like to have a sexual intercourse with her," he replies, "You mean, you're going to give me some trim?" (*CB* 239, 240), which is a linguistic regionalism once restricted to the South. The irony in a sexual relationship is expressed by the familiar but crude, "Whores were lying down first and getting up last . . . ." (*CB* 223). Homosexuality is alluded to in "That fool was as happy as a sissy in a CCC camp," (*CB* 189) a remark dating back to the Civilian Conservation Corps program of the 1930s. Angelou's streetwise mother also resorts sometimes to scatology. A lack of mercy is expressed by "Sympathy is next to shit in the dictionary, and I can't even read" (*CB* 175). Mother's advice about sex is "Keep your legs closed, and don't let nobody see your pocketbook" (*CB* 61). And she demands excellence: "Don't chippy at anything" (*CB* 69). Unscrubbed and suggestive language is used when

appropriate to a time and place. It establishes the tone of
the setting.

Angelou often incorporates rhetorical devices to produce
humor. Her creation of clever compound words ("a
firecracker July-the-Fourth burst") (*CB* 26); ("make-up
deep women") (*CB* 70); and of similes: "The giggles hung
in the air like melting clouds that were waiting on me" (*CB*
2); and ("I was young and crazy as a road lizard") (*GT* l2)
enrich her prose. Mother Vivian speaks light jive talk with
internal rhyme such as "I'm going to show you it ain't no
trouble when you pack double," (*CB* 229) encouraging her
daughter to handle two jobs. And she uses jive talk to
moan: "I can't win, 'cause of the shape I'm in" (*CB* l75).
These phrases again represent familiar folklore. Other
cultures have been recognized as employing similar
rhyming speech. Such language practice bonds and
develops unity within a given group. Rap music seems to
serve such a purpose.

Angelou's light poetry -- poetic entertainments -- is
laced with humor, which is derived from rhyme, some of
which is trite such as cake/steak; straw/raw; veal/zeal; and
help/kelp in "The Health Food Diner."[28] The last line of
each of the stanzas carries the humor. The obvious simple
rhymes convey a universal understanding.

In "Insomniac" Angelou delightfully notes how difficult
it sometimes is to go to sleep and in "The Telephone" she
comments on how dependent we are on it for social
sustenance.

In line 2 of "Harlem Hopscotch," Angelou alludes to a
joke that Langston Hughes says blacks tell on themselves:
"White is right/Yellow mellow/ But black get back!"[29] She
cleverly incorporates the race issue with the moves in a
game of hopscotch.

Angelou captures in "The Thirteens" (White) and "The Thirteens"(Black) the insult language of the "Dozens" so popular with young chanters although her lines seem less salacious than some of those commonly spoken on the street. The sound can be likened to a precursor of early Rap. Her black "Thirteens" lists the bitter realities of black street life in a manner that is matter-of-fact and accepting. Her white "Thirteens" by listing undesirable activites of that societal group emphasizes the hypocrisy of it all and once more points up the likenesses of one group with another.

A number of children's activities and responses have been handed down through the years in all cultures and are accepted as folk materials and light entertainments. Angelou includes in *Caged Bird* various chants, counting-rhymes, ring-songs, and tag-games which are common to recognized oral collections. The following nonsense rhyming chant is recalled as a tag-game song,

> Acka Backa, Sody Cracka
> Acka Backa, Boo
> Acka Backa, Sody Cracka
> I'm in love with you.   (*CB* ll5)

Dozens of analogues of the same chant with variant lines are quoted in the *Counting Out Rhymes Dictionary* edited by Roger D. Abrahams and Lois Rankin:

> Acker backer, soda cracker
> Acker backer boo.
> Acker backer, soda cracker,
> Out goes you.[30]

It is called a ring-game song in *American Negro Folklore*, edited by J. Mason Brewer:

Ooka dooka soda cracker
Does your father chew tobacco?
Yes my father chews tobacco
Ooka dooka soda cracker.[31]

It is also in *Jump-Rope Rhymes*, a dictionary edited by Roger D. Abrahams, as

Acca, bacca
Boom a cracka
Acca, bacca, boo.
If your daddy chews tobacco
He's a dirty-do.[32]

A relationship seems to exist between the Acca, bacca rhymes and Angelou's "Harlem Hopscotch." And so the variations go, crossing applications, decades, and ethnic lines. These inclusions reinforce Angelou's contention that we as people are more alike than unalike.

The *Book of Negro Folklore* includes a listing of play-songs and games. After chores in Stamps, Bailey and Maya would play hide and seek, and Bailey's voice would easily be identified calling the familiar play song:

Last night, night before,
Twenty-four robbers at my door
Who all is hid?
Ask me to let them in
Hit 'em in the head with a rollin' pin.
Who all is hid?   (*CB* 18)

These lines vary only slightly from its counterpart as it appears in the *Book of Negro Folklore*:

I got up about half-past four
Forty-four robbers was 'round my door

I opened the door and let 'em in
Hit 'em over the head with a rollin' pin.[33]

Iona and Peter Opie in *The Lore of Language of School
Children* include this song in the category of "nonsense
rhymes" and note three variants of it.

In the tradition of a folktale, the narrative of *Caged Bird*
opens with a poem, well-known to church members, that
children were often required to recite at the beginning of
religious services:

> What are you looking at me for?
> I didn't come to stay . . .;

This opening has been mentioned as universally appealing
to a broad audience, and serves to establish an immediate
rapport. Young Angelou is the speaker here. But as a
typical child, she requires prompting to elicit the next two
lines:

> I just come to tell you,
> It's Easter day.   (*CB* 1, 2)

All people can remember similar embarrassing situations in
childhood and a similar reaction of wanting to run and
hide.

Whether in poetry or prose, Angelou records the usual
spectrum of children's chants and games that are part of
our lore, jacks and hopscotch and the ring-game, all are
enjoyed by black children in Stamps. Bailey liked to play
mumbletypeg with the older boys. Both children enjoyed
hide and seek. The inclusion of these universal songs and
games shows that childhood days in Stamps were normal
and similar to the days of children everywhere. (Again the
more alike theme)

To conclude the discussion of wit and wisdom, there is little doubt Angelou's humor derives substantially from black folklore. This rich tradition does indeed enhance her narratives. With her unique presentation of stories, anecdotes, and poems, she successfully shows a community of song and laughter and courage, perhaps purposely contrived to demonstrate her people thriving in spite of the severe spartan living conditions and second-class citizenship status. Angelou is secure enough to laugh at her own weaknesses and at the flaws of her characters without humiliating anyone. Asimov has suggested "let us know each other's weaknesses and laugh at them, instead of hating them."[34] Maya Angelou acknowledges human weaknesses and balances stories of black endurance of oppression against white myths and misperceptions. With her injections of humor and Mother Wit, she succeeds in indicting institutionalized racism.

Notes

[1]Maya Angelou, *I Know Why the Caged Bird Sings* (New York: Random House, 1970) 76. Hereafter cited in the text as *CB*.

[2]Isaac Asimov, *Treasury of Humor* (Boston: Houghton, Mifflin, 1971) 345.

[3]Alan Dundes, "Introduction, " *Mother Wit from the Laughing Barrel* (Engelwood Cliff, New Jersey: Prentice-Hall, 1973) xiv.

[4]W. Edson Richmond, "Introduction," *Handbook of American Folklore*, ed. Richard M. Dorson (Bloomington, Indiana: Indiana University Press, 1983), *xii*.

[5]Quoted in Daryl Dance, *Shuckin' and Jivin'* (Bloomington: Indiana University Press, 1978) *xviii*.

[6]Dance *xviii.*

[7]Christie Davies, *Ethnic Humor Around the World* (Bloomington: Indiana University Press, 1990) 9.

[8]Asimov 317.

[9]Frederick Douglass, *Narrative of the Life of Frederick Douglass* (New York: Signet, 1968) 32.

[10]Joseph Boskin and Joseph Dorison, "Ethnic Humor: Subversion and Survival" in *American Humor*, Ed. Arthur Power Dudden (New York: Oxford University Press, 1987) 110.

[11]Boskin and Dorison 110.

[12]Maya Angelou, *Gather Together in My Name* (New York: Random House, 1974) 86. Hereafter cited in the text as *GT*.

[13]Asimov 311.

[14]Richard Dorson, ed. *Negro Folk Tales in Michigan* (Westport, Conn: Greenwood Press, 1986) 12.

[15]Dance.

[16]Trudier Harris, "Afro-American Humor," Colloquium, Arkansas State University, March 1986.

[17]Preacher stories continue to have popular appeal, even in comic strips. In a recent Snuffy Smith cartoon panel, a child's hand reaches from beneath a dinner table to take some food meant for a preacher. In another strip, a preacher invited to dinner declines because he has just finished eating, but designates his availability tomorrow night.

[18]A historian once complained that folktales always "belittle" authority figures, who are often depicted as fat and unattractive.

[19]Dorson 12.

[20]Langston Hughes, "Jokes Negroes Tell on Themselves," in *Mother Wit from the Laughing Barrel*, Ed. Alan Dundes (Engelwood Cliffs, N.J.: Prentice Hall, 1973) 638.

[21]Dorson 12.

[22]Davies 241.

[23]John Burma, "Humor as a Technique in Race Conflict," in *Mother Wit from the Laughing Barrel*, Ed. Alan Dundes (Engelwood Cliffs, N.J.: 1973) 627.

[24]Quoted in Burma 627.

[25]Langston Hughes and Arna Bontemps, ed., *Book of Negro Folklore* (New York: Dodd, Mead, 1958) 85.

[26]Burma 622, 625.

[27]Burma 625.

[28]Maya Angelou, *Maya Angelou Poems* (New York: Bantam 1986) 173.

[29]Langston Hughes, "Jokes," 639.

[30]Roger D. Abrahams and Lois Rankin, *Counting-Out Rhymes. A Dictionary* (Austin: University of Texas Press, 1980) 8.

[31]J. Mason Brewer, ed., *American Negro Folklore* (Chicago: Quadrangle Books, 1968) 373.

[32]Roger D. Abrahams, ed., *Jump-Rope Rhymes* (Austin: University of Texas Press, 1969) 5.

[33]Hughes and Bontemps 421.

[34]Asimov 212.

Chapter 3

The Autobiographies

The reader of the Angelou autobiographies is caught up and propelled onward by the subtle underlying sheer musicality of the prose and its organization. The importance of the gospel and blues rhythms has been noted in Chapter One, but there is a far more intriguing and covert application of familiar rhythms running throughout the series. This creates a comfort level by which a reader accepts and understands the growth of the prose from its *Caged Bird* homeyness to the swinging syncopations of *Gather Together* and *Singin' and Swingin* to the thoughtful ballad tones of *Heart of a Woman* and *All God's Children*. The simple chords and tinkling piano notes develop into warm, contemplative, impressive melodies. The reader has become a listener appreciative of what the tunesmith has to say.

The books replicate the performances of Angelou as she dances through life. A reader may sense the whirls of a waltz, the structure of a fox trot, the passion of a tango, the strut of a cake walk, the unbridled joy of jazz (swing), the sedate measures of a march. The Dance of Life for all of

us encompasses the movements incorporated within the
sentences of Maya Angelou.

The unifying themes and precedents for the five
Angelou autobiographies have been explored in Chapter
One, but each volume, though linked sequentially, has a life
of is own. And in the beginning is *Caged Bird.*

1. *I Know Why the Caged Bird Sings*
"Childhood Revisited"

The title of Angelou's first long book, *I Know Why the
Caged Bird Sings* (1970), was suggested by Abbey Lincoln
Roach. The approriateness of this borrowed line is most
apparent when it is considered in its original presentation.
It is taken from a line in Paul Laurence Dunbar's poem,
"Sympathy." Asked by an interviewer why does the caged
bird sing, Angelou replied,

> I think it was a bit of naivete or braggadoccio . . . to say
> I <u>know</u> why the caged bird sings! I was copying a Paul
> Laurence Dunbar poem so it's all right. I believe that a
> free bird . . . floats down, eats the early worm, flies away,
> and mates . . . . But the bird that's in a cage stalks up and
> down, looking constantly out . . . and he sings about
> freedom. Mr. Paul Laurence Dunbar says,
> > I know why the caged bird sings, ah me,
> >   when his wing is bruised and his bosom sore, --
> > When he beats his bars and he would be free;
> > It is not a carol of joy or glee,
> >   But a prayer that he sends from his heart's deep core,
> > But a plea, that upward to Heaven he flings --
> > I know why the caged bird sings![1]

The book's title cleverly attracts readers while subtly

reminding of the possibility of losing control or being denied freedom. Slaves and caged birds chirp their spirituals and flail against their constrictions.

I Know Why the Caged Bird Sings was an immediate commercial and critical success. Hailed as a "contemporary classic," it belongs in the "development genre," -- work in the tradition of *Bildungsroman* -- a subcategory of literature that focuses on growth and psychological development of the central figure. Transformation is the work's dominating theme, a metamorphosis of one who went from "being ignorant of being ignorant to being aware of being aware."[2] Throughout her writings, Angelou leaves a trail of overcoming parental and societal betrayal without espousing judgmental condemnations. Her maturation is shown by her responses to life's challenging situations.

According to Ernece B. Kelley, *Caged Bird* is a "poetic counterpart of the more scholarly *Growing up in the Black Belt: Negro Youth in the Rural South* by Charles S. Johnson.[3] Kelley calls *Caged Bird* an autobiographical novel rather than an autobiography for good reason: it reads like a novel. It has characters, plot, suspense, and denouement, although the form is episodic. Kelley believes, "On balance, *Caged Bird* is a gentle indictment of white American womanhood."[4] But Kelley's interpretation is too narrow. The stories, anecdotes, and jokes in *Caged Bird* do tell a dismaying story of white dominance, but Caged Bird in fact indicts nearly all of white society: American men, sheriffs, white con artists, white politicians, "crackers," uppity white women, white-trash children, all are targets. Their collective actions precipitate an outpouring of resentment from the African-American perspective. This suggests a thesis for examining *Caged Bird* through the lens of folklore and humor. It identifies the far broader picture of black America than its depicted focus.

Reviews of *Caged Bird* praise its use of words. E. M. Guiney wrote that "Angelou is a skillful writer, her language ranges from beautifully lyrical prose to earthy metaphor, and her descriptions have power and sensitivity. This is one of the best autobiographies of its kind that I have read."[5]   And R. A. Gross writes that "Her autobiography regularly throws out rich, dazzling images which delight and surprise with their simplicity."[6] Angelou's style demonstrates an obvious ease with vibrant language deployed for the most dramatic impact. A strong sense of the theatrical enriches the most pedestrian passages.

As of the mid 1980s, *Caged Bird* had gone through twenty hardback printings and thirty-two printings in paperback. Angelou's appearance at the 1993 Presidential Inauguration sent the book back to the top of the *New York Times* best seller lists and resulted in another round of printings. In fact, *Caged Bird* has never been out of print since first issued, nor it seems have any of her other books. That *Caged Bird* was once a selection of the Book of the Month Club, the Ebony Book Club, and also nominated for the National Book Award testifies to its appeal and broad popularity. *Caged Bird* alone would assure Angelou a place amongst America's most popular authors.

Angelou told Claudia Tate in an interview in 1983 that the occasion leading to the writing of *Caged Bird* was a dinner party in the late 1960s of Maya Angelou, James Baldwin (a much admired friend), and *Village Voice* cartoonist Jules Feiffer and his wife, Judy, at Feiffer's New York apartment.[7]   After a night of swapping anecdotes, someone suggested that Angelou had the material for a book from her experiences while growing up in Arkansas, Missouri, and California. The next day Judy Feiffer called an editor at Random House -- Robert Loomis -- to ask if he knew the poet Maya Angelou, who might be able to write an interesting book. Loomis called Angelou who demurred; she was tied up with a television project ("Black, Blues, Black"). Loomis called a few more times. When Angelou remained reluctant, Loomis conceded that perhaps it was just as well she did not attempt a book since autobiography was a most difficult form to handle, and it probably would be impossible to write one with any literary significance. This is a ploy that Angelou cannot resist, she has said. If someone suggests that she can't do something, she considers it a challenge and immediately accepts the proposal. She responded as expected to the reverse psychology and promised Loomis she would prepare a manuscript. Angelou wound up in London, closeting herself to work on the project. Nearly two years later, at a breakfast table, she confronted her good friend Jessica Mitford with a completed text. The two women spent the day poring over the manuscript, which Mitford found fascinating. *Caged Bird* was the resultant book. Over the years, Angelou has maintained a good working relationship with Robert Loomis, and he continued to serve as editor for all her Random House books. Loomis has made very few public comments on Angelou, as befits a professional editor, but in one instance did show an admiration for her craftsmanship by noting that she could completely reverse material, put the ending as the beginning, with no trouble whatsoever.

Memory plus distance equals true autobiography, the cliche reads. Benvenuto Cellini recommended that "all men of every sort should set forth their lives with their own hand; . . . But they should not commence so noble an undertaking before they have reached the age of forty years."[8] Since Angelou was almost forty when she undertook writing *Caged Bird*, she conforms to Cellini's caveat. According to Marcel Proust, memory can be a powerful weapon against mortality; for Angelou it is also a powerful weapon against bigotry.

With a mind filled with memories, Angelou recaptures her youth. She demonstrates an impressive recall of what it is like to be a child while diligently striving to maintain perspective. Some critics have questioned the point of view as being overly influenced by adult perception. Angelou has publicly addressed this difficulty and feels confident about her presentation. She structures her story into three parts: arrival, sojourn, and departure, geographically and psychologically. The narrative opens with a flashback to an Easter Sunday church scene in the early 1930s, shortly after her arrival from California. This scene constitutes a three-page prologue which establishes the insecurity and lack of status felt by the child Marguerite. She initially recreates the embarrassment she feels at her inability to remember the four-line poem she recites before the congregration, a situation often experienced by youngsters in like circumstances. As R. A. Gross says, Angelou "opens her autobiography and conveys the diminished sense of herself that pervaded much of her childhood."[9] Angelou recalls preparing for church and struggling with her troublesome body image. She is dressed in a discarded "ugly cut-down from a white woman's once-was-purple throwaway" (*CB* 2), which to her childish perception symbolizes her unacceptable being. She daydreams of having "real" hair and blue eyes, which, in her young mind, denote affluence and acceptability. A tone of "displaced" frustration pervades this introductory section, and the reader is immediately won over and becomes a sympathetic confidante. This beginning initiates the journey to establish a worthwhile self concept.

Following the church incident, Angelou begins the narrative proper and proceeds chronologically from her sojourn at Stamps to her introduction to San Francisco. The book ends with the birth of her son, symbolic of the end of childhood. However, this closing door opens a new status for the important women of *Caged Bird*: Angelou moves to the level of a mother; Vivian to that of grandmother; and Momma, while losing none of her wisdom, is less effective upon current life. A certain increase in worthiness accompanies motherhood and is an affirmation of Maya's value as a person. Angelou fleshes out the narrative of her very young days with stories that depict the humiliation and struggles resulting from the racism then practiced. Angelou recounts how difficult it was for hard-working African Americans to survive in an economically depressed and racially oppressed area. She intentionally incorporates incidents that show her community, in spite of its marginal existence, had moments of fun and laughter, and a significance as an entity.

In *I Know Why the Caged Bird Sings*, Angelou acknowledges that many strong memories of her childhood were of unpleasant happenings. However, she knows what a good solid sense of humor can contribute to the success of stories, and relies on her humor to soften her recollections. Making the difficult palatable allows for the incorporation of subtle judgments on the inequities of black, communal life. Thus while the comedy in *Caged Bird* and in her other writings is often dark humor emerging from hurt, it is woven into her narratives to do more than lighten them. Angelou's mother, Vivian, on a car ride to San Francisco, "strung humorous stories along the road like a bright wash and tried to captivate us" (*CB* 172). This bridging with humor by Vivian attempts to close the gap caused by her rather haphazard record of mothering. The many jokes, stories, anecdotes, and amusing incidents in Angelou's writings testify to a native humor and its bonding effect. Outsiders feel like insiders when they chuckle and smile together.

In a rather long and very impressive article, Elizabeth Schultz examines the classification of many African-American autobiographies. She particularly looks at the blues mode featured in these writings. Maya Angelou's *Caged Bird* is naturally included by Schultz as a blues genre autobiography, as discussed in a previous chapter. Schultz does state that "Black autobiography has a testimonial as well as a blues mode."[10] Thus there is a blending of two differing approaches to autobiography by most black writers, particularly of more recent times, according to Schultz. The single, individual voice is seen to expand and reflect a communal tone to impact upon the reader. Testimonial autobiographies often shift chronology, as Angelou does with her church-scene opening of *Caged Bird*, to affect later experiences. The mixture of blues and testimonial offers a counterpoint presentation of personal convictions and confrontations balanced against the innate wit and grace essential to survival. The dependence upon a black generated folklore and humor has already been explored. Schultz goes on to note that blues autobiographers are involved in a process of self-discovery.[11] They are too involved with life events and responses for reflection, but their readers are drawn into this relationship.[12] Angelou is perceived as writing from a "perch of time," allowing her a perspective of maturity.[13] The vision of the black autobiographer, particularly in the blues mode, is shaped by the writer's experience in his community and a discovery of a personal consciousness, according to Schultz.[14] This approach depends upon a level of maturity for assessing the good and the bad and expressing the hope that the good will prevail.

Angelou's style in *Caged Bird* reflects the inflections

and rhythms and natural metaphors of the blues which creates a sense of community with her readers, but she also incorporates prose identifiable with African-American sermoninizing. This, too, signifies to her particular audience.[15] An essential blues characteristic of ironic understatement serves as a vehicle for enduring the contradictions of life. Yet, conscious overstatement of episodic details allows a focus upon the extreme emotional responses.[16] Angelou permits herself flights of fantasy and exaggeration to express an intensity of feeling.[17] This is particularly pertinent to *Caged Bird* where a major goal is self-determination.

Caged Bird chronicles approximately ten years that Angelou and her brother Bailey, Jr. live with their paternal grandmother, Mrs. Annie Henderson, who owns the store in the segregated section of Stamps, Arkansas. Marguerite and Bailey, Jr. had been tagged and shipped by their parents by rail from California to Arkansas to live with Momma. Mrs. Henderson's world "was bordered on all sides with work, duty, religion, and 'her place'" (*CB* 47). "Momma" Henderson and her views on life provide what little stability Maya experiences.

In 1935, "without warning," father Bailey Johnson, Sr. swoops into town from California, and Marguerite and Bailey, Jr. are again uprooted and taken to live with their mother in St. Louis. Here Angelou meets the maternal side of her family and finds these relatives to be an extremely close-knit group: "Grandfather had a famous saying that caused great pride in his family: "Bah, Jesus, I live for my wife, my children and my dog" (*CB* 50). Angelou actively advocates family strength and cohesion as often as possible. Her maternal grandmother, a quadroon or an octoroon, raised in a German setting, is an active force in local politics. Grandfather Baxter was a dark West Indian native in stark contrast to his wife's nearly white visage. Each had the distinctive dialect of their backgrounds. However, the grandmother's German upbringing and light appearance made her more acceptable to the local power structure and assured her a position of significance.

But the urban high-life differs diametrically from the fundamentalist structure of rural Stamps. In St. Louis, Marguerite is raped by her mother's current paramour while she is under his care. The detailed recall of the rape itself and the searing memory of it inform the reader of the tremendous impact both mental and physical upon the innocent victim. On the courtroom stand at the trial of the accused, a Mr. Freeman, Angelou hides previous advances made by him -- some innocent and some not-so-innocent -- still fearful of his threats. As a result, he is given a reduced sentence. The rape of a black child is apparently not of great concern to the judicial system of that time and place. The lifetime impact upon the small victim apparently does not warrant serious punishment. But his immediate release proves to be his undoing. Street justice is exercised with no ensuing legal recourse. He is found dead, possibly kicked to death by Angelou's "mean and ugly" uncles, righting a family wrong and asserting its status. The eight-year old child associates his death with her lack of truthfulness and therefore blames herself. She takes upon herself the guilt for the lawless act of retribution. Speech causes tragedy, she concludes simplistically, so to avoid further harm to anyone, Marguerite decides to stop talking except to her trusted brother, Bailey. Her mother mistakes this retreat into silence for impudence, however, and ships the two children back to Stamps and the strict discipline and uncomplicated protection of Grandmother Henderson.

Shortly thereafter, in the General Store Marguerite meets Mrs. Flowers, her community's annointed intellectual, who becomes Angelou's "first life line" (*CB* 77). Momma solicits her aid with the mute Maya, and at her sanctuary-like home Mrs. Flowers gently and graciously draws out Marguerite and encourages her to continue an interest in literature. Mrs. Flowers extolls the value of poetry: "Poetry is music written for the human voice. Until you read it (aloud), you will never love it."[18] Through this device, reciting poetry aloud to herself, Angelou regains her use of speech. A love of literature and literacy deepens at this time and continues throughout her life. According to Francoise Lionnet-McCumber, Angelou makes reference to over 100 different literary characters in her autobiographies,[19] attesting to her familiarity with conventional literature. Angelou's devotion to learning -- to literacy -- addresses what Robert B. Stepto says is "the central myth of black culture in America: 'the quest for freedom and literacy.'"[20] African Americans hungered for these goals and strove mightly in many subtle ways to attain them.

The pursuit of knowledge in Angelou's early development, according to George E. Kent, draws on "two areas of black life: the religious and the blues traditions." Her grandmother represents the religious influence: Black Fundamentalism, the Christian Methodist Episcopal (CME) Church. Her mother, on the other hand, stands for the "blues-street tradition," the fast life.[21] Francoise Lionnet-McCumber in her dissertation adds a third term to this comparison: "the literary tradition, all the fictional works that the narrator reads avidly."[22] *Caged Bird* draws heavily upon these elements: the hundred references noted above, a couple of dozen biblical quotes, and the music felt throughout.

Following Angelou's re-awakening and emergence under the guidance of her mentor, Mrs. Flowers, *Caged*

Bird's narrative moves forward, incorporating stories that
show what it is to be black in the American South.
Angelou's rural family associations are typical of the time
and place. She tells of an ecumenical church revival
meeting that reflects the religious cooperation and
involvement of the entire community. Familiar evening
entertainments often revolved around ghost stories which
were told to both skeptical and supportive superstitious
listeners. The folkloric derivations of these activities have
been previously addressed in detail. Other reports of daily
activities reflect life for African Americans in Stamps,
Arkansas and the hundreds of other Stamps.

In 1940, Angelou is graduated with honors from
Lafayette County Training School. She recalls with
considerable dismay that the commencement speaker -- a
white politician -- promises academic improvements for
white schools and the continuation of athletic programs for
blacks: "The white kids were going to have a chance to
become Galileos and Madame Curies and Edisons and
Gauguins, and our boys (the girls weren't even in on it)
would try to be Jesse Owenses and Joe Louises" (*CB* 151).
A graduation scene appears in many autobiographies as
signifying survival and achievement. Angelou finds her
graduation experience once again points to how opportunity
for African Americans is limited and stereotyped by the
white patriarchal society. However, the singing of the
Negro national anthem, James Weldon Johnson's "*Lift Ev'ry
Voice and Sing*," expresses a unity and portends hope for
the future.

Soon thereafter, an increasingly venturesome teenage
Bailey, Jr. encounters his first slain black man. Momma
Henderson decides it would be safer and timely for the
children to be with their parents in California. So
Marguerite departs for California with Momma, Bailey to

follow. Maya, Bailey, and Momma live together briefly in Los Angeles. Vivian takes the children to Oakland, and Momma returns to Stamps. Vivian remarries and the family resettles in San Francisco. Angelou attends George Washington High School days and studies dance at the California Labor School at night. Maya goes to spend some time with her father and his lady in southern California. She accompanies Bailey, Sr. on a wild jaunt to a Mexican village where he seems to be known. When he becomes too drunk to drive back home, Marguerite takes the wheel, even though she had no driving instruction. She somewhat successfully maneuvers the two of them to the border, where Bailey, Sr. revives and can again take over. This incident furthers her growing awareness that she can indeed do anything she sets her mind to, as Mother Vivian regularly extolls.

After a run-in with her father's mistress, Angelou leaves their home and strikes out on her own. She lives for a time in a junk yard with other homeless adolescents. They -- "a collage of Negro, Mexican and White" -- become her family. The great importance of this "family," Liliane K. Arensburg finds is "that these children disprove the racial prejudice -- and its concurrent death fantasies -- of her earlier experiences."[23] Angelou becomes aware that an African American can survive and bond with like-kind of other races. The unquestioning support of each other in this group allows Angelou to reach beyond her former boundaries and attitudes. One of the group lives in a real home and allows its use by the entire band for periodical, personal hygiene. Rules are practical and accepted by all. They share a common goal of survival. This sharing required for survival was tested by Thor Heyerdahl, the explorer, when he deliberately mixed varied ethnic personalities on one of his expeditions. He found their only

differences arose from minor personal traits rather than their
ethnicity. They were able to adjust to the common bounds
of necessity. A former sequestered juror from a major
murder trial when questioned about racial problems in the
jury room replied that the only problems arose from
irritating personal traits, not race, thus further attesting to
the ability of diverse persons to form bonds when faced
with a common situation.

Angelou eventually returns to San Francisco to live
again with her mother. As a maturing teenager, she begins
to awaken sexually. Uncertain about her sexuality and
fearful of being unwomanly, she turns to her mother, who
tries to reassure her. But her lack of development and new,
unfamiliar emotional responses leave her still curious and
ambivalent. So Angelou challenges her womanhood
forthrightly by instigating a casual sexual encounter. She
becomes pregnant, keeps her situation hidden from all for
over eight months, and just as she graduates from high
school announces her condition to her family. School
records show her dropping out of school one semester but
returning to graduate from Mission High School after a
summer session. Very shortly thereafter she gives birth to
her son, Clyde (Guy).

The characters on the pages of *Caged Bird* are fully
developed and three-dimensional. The only perceivable
distortion might be that literary license seems to embellish
them somewhat to larger-than-life personalities. However,
they are real-life flesh and blood people who were a part of
the life of Maya Angelou. Angelou, the principal personage
of *Caged Bird*, assumes two personae: the voice of "Ritie"
(a diminutive of Angelou's first name, Marguerite) who
describes poignantly the incidents in her childhood and
adolescence; and the voice of Maya, the near adult who is
somewhat introspective, more objective and less personal.

Angelou uses the second voice to make general observations or to editorialize. For example, when Uncle Willie hides from the prowling klansmen, the Maya voice objects to the lack of police protection for African Americans against obviously lawless activities.

In Jungian archetypal terms, Angelou is the anima. The animus -- the male part of her make-up -- is represented by her brother Bailey. Bailey Johnson, Jr. is a firm, rather free-spirited youngster who because of being male, is able to move about in his segregated   world with fewer restrictions than sister Maya. The two children are very close, probably because of their life situations as much as from their shared experiences and interests. They are both highly literate and adaptable. Bailey is protective of Maya, yet each appears to be very independent. Bailey must face greater dangers in the larger white-dominated world and is taught early on of the risks of being an African-American man. He does not allow this to prevent his functioning as a typical bright, energetic boy. He, more than any other character, with his outgoing personality and natural curiosity seems to exemplify Angelou's contention regarding blacks and whites: that they are more alike than un-alike; that there are more similarities than differences. Bailey likes reading, comic books, movies, sportscasts, following around his St. Louis uncles and a little strutting. He idolizes his attractive, devil-may-care mother. All of these things could be said about any boy of his age. However, the promise of Bailey the boy seems to have been blunted for Bailey the man who wound up in prison. This is a sad, unfortunate development, but is no' openly attributed to race. His embracing the street-style is accepted as a matter of circumstance and choice.

In addition to Bailey, whom the young Angelou acclaims the greatest person in her world, most male

characters in *Caged Bird* receive exceptionally sympathetic
treatment: there are the "dirt-disappointed" field workers,
whose efforts weren't enough "no matter how much cotton
they had picked" (*CB* 7); there is Daddy Clidell, a
successful businessman; Grandfather Baxter, a family man
of stature who had "mean" (tough) but not cruel sons; Uncle
Willie, handicapped physically but not mentally; and Mr.
McElroy who owned property. He was an "independent
Black man, a near anachronism in Stamps" (*CB* 17). Even
Mr. Freeman, the rapist of a child, had worldly status and
held an important position with the railroad.   In an
interview with Claudia Tate Angelou said that she "wanted
people to see that the man was not totally an ogre." These
men all evidence strength and some attainment, even the
worst of them. This would appear to be a conscious effort
to   minimize   popular   negative   images   of   the
African-American male.

Angelou's father, Bailey, Sr., does not fare so well.
Here the personal outweighs the general. She confesses that
"(her) father had not shown any particular pride in (her) and
very little affection" (*CB* 195). Thus he is a "stranger" to
her and someone to whom she did not feel any loyalty. His
betrayal of the children was evidenced by his appearance in
their lives only at times of moving them around -- out of
his way and responsibility. Her father lived in a fast lane
characteristic of "hipster" types. In *Caged Bird* and in a
later book, Angelou ridicules her father's speech habit of
"er-er-ing" and his tendency to posture. Bailey, Sr. has all
the earmarks of a blow-hard. He wheels in and out of her
early life with a lot of "pizazz," but little substance. He
does not fill a major role, as a father should, but is seen
more as a biological acknowledgment. Even he, however,
survives and flourishes in his world, despite Angelou's low
opinion of him. This lack of regard for Bailey, Sr. did not

prevent Angelou from acknowledging the importance of a father figure to a family. Until her son is accepted as a grown man, she searches unsucessfully for a man who would be a proper father and role model for him. She encounters only more betrayal.

Angelou's treatment of female role models in *Caged Bird* -- of her Mrs. Flowers and of her mother and grandmothers -- is even more positive than her treatment of African-American males. Since it is generally accepted that children of her era developed stronger bonds with their mother than their father, it is not surprising to find Angelou emphasizing the importance of mother and grandmothers. Such emphasis on mothers is, according to Stephanie A. Demetrakopoulos, "typical in women's autobiography due to the innate and archetypal aspects of the women's psyche, celebrated and codified long ago as the Eleusinian Mysteries."[24] These archetypal aspects may be incorporated in women's autobiographies, but it does not seem to be done consciously by Angelou. What she does do consciously, however, is to make an effort to counter unflattering female types described in the earlier literature by James Fenimore Cooper and Washington Irving. In this literature, grandmother matriarchs are depicted as silent, post-forty, corpulent and passively working in the kitchen.[25]

Compared to these earlier female stereotypes, Angelou's paternal grandmother, Mrs. Henderson, is a symbol of strength; she is in no way a weak, passive personality. She is not silent. She is the moral center and the voice of authority in *Caged Bird*. She is an Earth Mother, a figure who is good, kind, nurturing, and protecting. Angelou calls her "Momma" and in fiction she would be the "Madonna" figure, one who stands for love and home. Her love for Angelou is unconditional and maternal. This love contrasts markedly with the paternal, in which love is more conditional and is usually earned and given only if one is obedient and attractive. In Angelou's extended family an atmosphere of warmth and love prevails that is not bestowed as a result of obedience or something earned. The strong maternal instinct enveloped all.

Momma Henderson, for all her matriarchal positioning, is a total realist. If she ever failed to do her duty or did not observe her place as a lower class citizen, she knows the white power structure would soon find a way to express its displeasure. Those in control are generally more interested in order than in justice. Momma's firm leadership while still being forced to keep her place, sends a mixed message to the younger generation that required a good deal of maturity and distancing for them to understand. It was some time before Angelou expressed, particularly in her poetry, the courage and patience of those who kept quiet and saw to the survival of those in whom the future rested.

Two other characteristics of Momma contrast with the matriarchs found in early American literature. Inasmuch as there were few or no opportunities in the professions, many women turned to religion as a means of escape from the confinement of their defined roles. Thus, Momma, a natural leader, became an important figure in her church. Moreover, Momma was an entrepreneur, a female rarity in the 1930s and unheard of one hundred years earlier. Her business acumen helped her family survive the depression and keep off relief; she preserved their independence. This would not be a role natural to her predecessors.

In addition to her praise of Momma Henderson, Angelou expresses great pride in her maternal grandmother, Mrs. Baxter, who did not take a back seat to anybody. As previously noted, she was very light-skinned and probably could have easily passed as white. She chose to remain a part of a black community. She and her family spoke standard English and provided important liaison with the local white power structure. She was a political activist who wielded considerable clout in her neighborhood in St. Louis, thus giving the lie to the myth that African Americans could not participate effectively in the political arena. Power blocks delivered votes and reaped the rewards. The Baxters understood the strength of unity.

Similarly, Angelou's mother, Vivian Baxter Johnson, emerges as an extremely vital personality. She is Angelou's role model. Angelou absorbs her personal philosophy and frequently quotes her maxims of life. Mrs. Johnson's beauty and zest when she was young "made her powerful and her power made her unflinchingly honest" (CB 174); and "To describe (her) would be to write about a hurricane in its perfect power. Or the climbing, falling colors of a rainbow" (CB 49). Vivian is a city woman and sees no need in her world to conform to the subservient country folk tradition. She can sing and swing at will.

Vivian also found it too inconvenient to care for her two children or found it too incompatible with her life style. She finds an excuse -- a depressed Maya -- to send Maya and Bailey back to Stamps. This cavalier dumping of her children appears to Stephanie Demetrakopoulos as a failure to come to terms with the matriarchate (her mother), and this treatment, Demetrakopoulos finds, is a disturbing weakness of the book. Angelou's mother is seen as "shockingly callous" and insensitive by sending the little girl back to Stamps after being raped. Maya is traumatized by events and full of unwarranted guilt. The mother's behavior here and at other times does not justify the favorable treatment she got from Angelou and this action, Demetrakopoulos says, is "puzzling and unsettling."[26] Vivian is just as guilty as Bailey, Sr. of betraying their children. But Mother Vivian is idolized by both Johnson

children and neither would dream of questioning her
less-than perfect mothering. She is all that is glamorous
and movie-life desirable to them. In Angelou's next book,
Gather Together in My Name, she does question her
mother's sense of responsbility. She wonders whether her
mother " . . . who had left (her) with others until she was
thirteen . . . (would) feel more responsibility for (her) child
Guy (nee Clyde) than she had felt for her own" (GT 3).
Thus there existed an awareness of an imperfect relationship
with mother as well as father. Even if not openly
acknowledged, this would have a dire effect upon sense of
worth. Angelou always seems to seek out her mother's
wisdom and advice, however, and gives her an important
role in her life. She does not seem to dwell upon any
rejection or lack of love. Years later Vivian would move
in with Maya, who would never abdicate family
responsibility without remorse. She, like Momma
Henderson, fully understood and accepted motherhood and
its attendant Madonna aspects.

In *Caged Bird* and her other autobiographies, Angelou
does discover herself and her capabilities and effectively
conveys her personality and opinions. Her real purpose in
Caged Bird, however, as well as in her other books, is to
illuminate and explain her race's condition by protesting
against white misconceptions and legitimatizing the
extremes sometimes required for survival. While justifying
some questionable activities, she does not judge the right or
wrong of them. She wants to destroy those stereotyped
images of African Americans that prevailed when she wrote
Caged Bird. Angelou rightly resents this thinking that
dehumanized her people, and which continued to be
practiced despite civil rights progress. Instead of writing an
argumentative response or preaching to protest, Angelou
chose the traditional form of autobiography to dramatize the

conditions, presenting easily understood counter-examples. The reader can relate and conclude that the stereotype image is false and destructive. Forces beyond control dictate actions determined to be anti-social. Given equal opportunities, Angelou believes that like reactions would be demonstrated by blacks and whites. Later she acted this out as the white queen in Genet's *The Blacks*.

Caged Bird ends with Angelou facing the adult world full of "Mother Wit" and determination. She accepts enthusiastically the challenge of sustaining herself and her son. Her focus is that of a mature, responsible young woman. She will do better than her predecessors and enhance the mantle of motherhood. She has gained strength from her adversities, and increased status as a mother gives her added confidence for the future. The Maya character in *Caged Bird* addressed the author's stated themes by overcoming many obstacles, establishing some sense of self as a mother, and repeatedly emphasizing the importance of literacy and education. She also serves the traditional black autobiographical themes of bondage, her dependence on others; flight, as she breaks out on her own with the junk yard group; and freedom, by taking control of her life. Thus Angelou includes all required elements in *Caged Bird* and uses it as the base for her future books.

2. *Gather Together in My Name*
"Picking the Way"

The success of *Caged Bird* encouraged Angelou to continue her life story. Her second volume, *Gather Together in My Name* (1974), took three-and-a-half years to

write and continues the saga of adventures in California,
taking up from where *Caged Bird* ends. *Gather Together*
is a travel story. An apt title for the book could be
"Travels with Maya." Her experiences carry her from San
Francisco to Los Angeles to San Diego to Stamps back to
San Francisco to Stockton and finally to Oakland, all in a
brief time-span.

In these travels, Angelou once more exposes her
audience to a varied cast, including a fair share of criminal
types. The following questionable operators populate her
book: L. D. Tolbrook, a pimp and con-man; Beatrice and
Johnnie May, lesbians and prostitutes; Troubadour Martin,
a dealer in stolen goods; Big Mary, who kidnaps Angelou's
son; and a sundry sprinkling of junkies. Angelou skirts the
edge of the underworld, but her innocence and openness
bring out the good in unsavory people, and they keep her
from personal harm. Her life is actually enriched by her
encounters with the fringes of society.

Reviewers found merit in the new volume. Phoebe
Adams, for example, in *Atlantic*, said *Gather Together* was
"excellently written."[27] The *Library Journal* reviewer
commented that it was "tremendously moving,"[28] and
Choice felt that Angelou was a "fine story teller."[29] A
disquieting note, however, was expressed by Selwyn Cudjoe
who thought that while *Gather Together* was well-written,
better written than *Caged Bird*, it does not succeed because,
unlike *Caged Bird*, it lacks "moral weight and an ethical
center," thus denying it an organizing principle and rigor
capable of keeping the work together:

> If I may be permitted, the incidents of the book appear
> merely gathered together in the name of Maya Angelou.
> They are not so organized that they may achieve a complex
> level of signification. In fact, it is the absence of these

qualities which make the work conspicuously weak.[30]

Cudjoe's criticism seems forced and his opinions are couched in bloated language: "complex level of signification." In spite of Cudjoe's captious comment, a moral center is present. As noted, many incidents involve unsavory characters and even criminal behavior: lesbians, pimps, prostitution, drugs, love affairs, stolen goods, etc., but poetic justice is eventually rendered and right prevails. These people are not winners. However, there may be a moral weakness in that these lifestyles are not roundly condemned but matter of factly acknowledged. In this raffish milieu, Angelou serves what some critics have called a picaresque literary figure -- a carefree, fun-loving individual -- who moves through a sleazy world with good intentioned determination and emerges stronger for the exposure. The existence of evil does not imply all things are evil nor that it must triumph. In fact, evil does not triumph in *Gather Together*. The innocent, Angelou, emerges triumphant.

The narrative organization in *Gather Together* follows the format found in *Caged Bird*. The book evolves as a series of interrelated episodes rather than as a single straight-line narrative. Once again, a series of incidents are chronologically tied together to describe Angelou's quest for survival and identity.

In an interview published in *Black Women Writers at Work* Angelou noted that the title of *Gather Together* has a "biblical origin."[31] It is a "New Testament injunction for the travailing soul to pray and commune while waiting patiently for deliverance."[32] As for the motive for writing the unvarnished experiences in *Gather Together*, Angelou has said,

> . . . comes from the fact that I saw so many adults lying to
> so many young people, lying in their teeth, saying 'You
> know, when I was young, I never would have done . . .
> Why I couldn't . . . I shouldn't . . . .' Lying. Young
> people know when you're lying; so I thought for all those
> parents and non-parents alike who have lied about their
> past, I will tell it.[33]

The underlying deep structure of this statement of
motive carries four interesting implications: One is that
people -- young or old, white or black -- are hypocritical.
It is proverbial that what people say and what they do more
often than not conflict.   Kierkegaard, the philosopher and
theologian, pointed out that hypocrisy is so deeply ingrained
in man's nature that a man could lose his hypocrisy about
as easily as a fish could lose its scales.   Angelou should be
commended for facing and reporting repugnant situations
truthfully.   She chooses not to whitewash the real world she
encountered.   But she conveys the positive message of hope
by proving an exposure to the dark side need not cause a
loss of faith and goodness.

Angelou is also following an old religious custom,
described by a theological term -- exomologesis -- in which
a person expresses "complete openness about his life, past
and present, followed by important personal changes, with
the support and encouragement of other members of the
congregation."[34]   Writing *Gather Together* when she is in
her mid-forties, the Cellini approved age and perspective,
and having been frank previously about her life experiences
in *Caged Bird*, Angelou is, nevertheless, worried about
public reaction to an even more candid recounting of the
adventures of a "reckless" and "foolish" young girl.   A
strong enough concern existed that Angelou admits to
conferring with her son, her mother, and her brother to
solicit their comments.   She said, "This is what I want to

do. I want to say to young people 'You may encounter many defeats, but you must not be defeated.'" Then she read her family salient chapters, and they all expressed unconditional support. Her mother told her, "Write it." Her brother said, "Please tell it." Despite their approval and encouragement, this book was even more painful to write than *Caged Bird*, she says, "because it deals with unsavory parts of my past."[35] But it makes more powerful her message of survival. These events happened when she was in control of her life and the choices were hers. However, providing sustenance for herself and her son led to some of the quick and easy choices.

A third implication is that Angelou wants to anticipate any criticism of her past life. By including unpleasant as well as pleasant incidents, she can head off negative comment from anyone who might be inclined to bring up something unfavorable or scandalous. "Yah, I knew her when," someone might say, and thus destroy her credibility. By taking the offensive with full, open disclosure, Angelou stares down her detractors. She gains an edge with her readers and they are more receptive to accepting her material as gospel.

There is finally, a fourth practical reason for her candor: sex sells, as romance novel publishers and tabloid journalists can attest. And there was a desire to meet the initial sales figures of *Caged Bird*. Since Angelou's descriptions of her experiences as a sometime prostitute and as a short-term brothel operator, as related in this book, are virtually voyeuristic, she distances herself from blatant participation. She manages to maintain for her persona the traditional view that sex and love go together, whether it is in a brothel or in the privacy of one's own bedroom. Angelou is removed from any stigma that might result from crass participation. She humanizes her involvement and realizes wrong doing, asking for forgiveness for youthful poor judgment.

Gather Together, a chronicle of another segment of the author's daily travails, is a further journey seeking solutions. It concludes with the inevitable realization by Angelou that the answers are within herself. As mentioned, *Gather Together* follows the same format as *Caged Bird*: a "preface" presents the problem and sets the scene. This is, of course, the traditional structure associated with testimonial autobiographies as previously discussed in references to the Schultz article. The situation presented finds Maya Angelou, black, female, and an unmarried mother with a two-month old son to support. She is without any funds or job skills. She is 17 years old and has just graduated from high school. The place is San Francisco, and the time is the mid 1940s, just after the end of World War II. During the war years, the mood was upbeat. The law of supply and demand meant that good paying jobs existed for all people, anyone willing to try and learn. There was little talk of prejudice. Now with the end of the war, defense plants have shut down and soldiers who had been released from service hang around "the ghetto corners like forgotten laundry left on a backyard fence."[36] There had been a lengthy feast but inexorably the famine must follow. The job market tightens and easy money dries up. Making a living, honest or otherwise, becomes a fierce challenge.

Having a young child to care for means that further education may not be feasible for the single parent Angelou. Her mother and stepfather, Daddy Clidell, however, do offer to care for her son if she decides to continue her education in college. But Angelou is concerned and reluctant to relinquish her maternal role. She recalls her childhood and wonders if her mother would really accept responsibility for Clyde (Guy). She ends her prefatory section, as in *Caged Bird*, with reflection: "The mixture of arrogance and insecurity is as volatile as the much-touted alcohol and gasoline. The difference is that with the former there is a long internal burning usually terminating in self-destroying implosion" (*GT* 5).

In *Gather Together*, Angelou is still involved with her themes of protest and survival; of protest against prejudice, which shines more lightly upon the male and the white; of the need to survive and raise her son in a world dominated by the "loathsome white." The mysterious ways of whites continue to disconcert her as they did in *Caged Bird*, reflecting her rural community perceptions. Her mother, grandmother, and her personal experiences all educate her about whites, but do nothing to lessen her aggravation or to develop within her an acceptance of feeling or acting inferior. During this period, she learns that it is white men who ask prostitutes to do "nasty things." Furthermore, white folks are vulgar, and white men are sad as lovers (*GT* 141). Angelou writes that the examiner for a test she takes for a telephone job is "A silly white woman who probably counted on her toes" (*GT* 6). Angelou's own prejudices crop up frequently as conditioned responses without consideration of their limitations. Her comments in *Gather Together* counter her junk yard lessons of *Caged Bird*. Keep in mind that the books are reflective of a particular period in Angelou's growth and development. *Gather Together* covers about four years of youthful maturation.

Angelou did absorb many of her mother's warnings that enable her to function in the general white world. Angelou, her mother cautioned, should avoid "speaking to whites, and especially white men" (*GT* 50), an admonition that echoes what she had learned earlier in Stamps and had reported in *Caged Bird*: "the less you say to white-folks or even powhitetrash) the better" (*CB* 22). Her mother also warns her that "When a white man sees your teeth he thinks he sees your underclothes" (*GT* 51). Angelou does find some positive black and white interactive behavior to report. This presages an eventual acceptance of individual actions. She even expresses tolerance of many things and certainly of all levels of language. One thing Angelou will not tolerate, however, is the use of the word "nigger" under any circumstances. The disparagement implied in the word is deeply ingrained, whether in a rural or urban setting. The prohibition is sometimes lifted in dialectic reporting of black-on-black conversation, but purely for purposes of realism.

A key incident in *Gather Together* occurs halfway through the book. It is another confrontation scene -- a redux of the confrontation scenes with Angelou and Mrs. Cullinan; and of Momma and the dentist in *Caged Bird*. This time it is a confrontation with a clerk in a general merchandise store in Stamps when Angelou returns to visit Grandmother Henderson. Southern blacks were still expected to defer to whites at that time and in that place. But when an adult Angelou is again misnamed -- "This one's Margaret or Marjorie or something like that" (*GT* 76) -- this sets Angelou off, and she responds impulsively, impudently, and imprudently: "I'll slap you into the middle of next week if you even dare to open your mouths again" (*GT* 77).

Angelou's grandmother learns about the incident from a telephone call and confronts Angelou with an admonition in language characteristic of her background: ". . . you was downtown showing out" (*GT* 78). It was a matter of principle, Angelou replies. Momma answers by swinging her hand hard against Angelou's cheek, saying, "Here's your principle," (*GT* 78), which demonstrates the firm discipline used to insure safety to African-American offspring. But Angelou had wanted to show that her community also had a code of proper behavior. Momma had lived a long time in a segregated community. She knows the local white thinking and warns Angelou, again in moving, informal, elliptical language that Angelou captures so accurately,

> You think 'cause you've been to California these crazy
> people won't kill you? You think them lunatic cracker
> boys won't try to catch you in the road and violate you?
> You think because of your all-fired principle some of the
> men won't feel like putting their white sheets on and riding
> over here to stir up trouble? You do, you're wrong. Ain't
> nothing to protect you and us except the Good Lord and
> some miles.   (*GT* 78-79)

In addition to her other qualities, Momma is a practical and prudent person. Angelou's story shows how dangerous life could be for African Americans. One could get killed in Stamps, Arkansas, for simply "showing out," just like Emmett Till did in Mississippi for his innocent remark to a salesgirl.

The principle that Angelou felt was challenged was that her "personhood was violated." As Hannah Nelson observes,

> The most important thing about black people is that they
> don't think they can control anything except their own
> persons. So everything black people think and do has to be
> understood as very personal. As a result, the inviolability
> of the Afro-Americans's personhood is so closely guarded
> that any assault upon his/her person is frequently resisted.[37]

African Americans are often accused of being "too touchy" or "too sensitive" when they react to situations as Angelou did, but the accusers are generally ignorant of the depth of the cultural issue involved. Generally, bad treatment and the lack of conventional courtesy is rightly considered a personal affront by the targets but rarely by the perpetrators. This is magnified in interracial settings. Momma then packs up Angelou's belongings and Angelou returns to her mother and son in San Francisco. The door is closed in Stamps, Arkansas. Angelou belongs to a wider world and never again sees her grandmother Henderson, but will forever carry Momma's marks.

As the principal personage of *Gather Together*, Angelou is still the youthful, high-spirited Marguerite, -- "Ritie' -- Johnson. Again writing from the advantage of maturity, Angelou recounts those confused adolescent years of 17 to 19, as she entered the real world, determined to make her own way. These *are* adolescent years, and Angelou describes some foolish mundane little things she did like wearing too much makeup. And she sees herself as a product of "Hollywood upbringing and (her) own romanticism" (*GT* 27). These are typical, trivial teen-age concerns. They are normal considerations as contrasted to the abnormal underworld activities with which she finds herself involved. Her teenage heart and dreams must cope with adult arenas. The difficult task of sustaining independence means compromising her dreams.

Although Angelou briefly flirts with criminal deeds, she finds rationalization in her need to make a living for her son and herself. She is always aware of being outside society's norms and admits that during these times she slid "down into the slimy world of mortal sin" (*GT* 140). She bounces from "unpleasant pillar to illegal post," to use the words of Phoebe Adams in the *Atlantic*,[38] but always as a temporary means to an acceptable end. Angelou does not lose her moral compass and maintains a firm distinction between right and wrong.

What emerges in *Gather Together* is an Angelou who is resourceful, capable, and tough-minded. She realizes that there is no free lunch and asks no quarter. She will take on any challenge to survive and feels that she can apply her intelligence to any reasonable task. She neither understands nor accepts failure. She will tackle whatever comes her way. A lack of experience in Creole cooking does not stop her from taking such a job and doing it well. Dance routines she performs with R. L. Poole, although "largely unappreciated" by audiences (*GT* 113), are nevertheless moderately successful and serve as preparation for future acceptance at the Purple Onion night club. Variety of employment is no barrier to Angelou. She sees opportunity where others might see oppression.

Angelou does not feel that her education ended with graduation from high school. Having been encouraged early in her life to appreciate literature, she continues to read, as she had done since childhood: "until the gray light entered (her) room" (*GT* 59). As a result, she becomes a wide reader with an inquisitive mind and a confidence in her own perceptions. Her reading was apparently eclectic and of college calibre: from the poetry of Countee Cullen to the lengthy prose of Russian authors. She refuses to be limited or "caged."

At the end of relating an anecdote, Angelou often generalizes about her experience, a practice she started in *Caged Bird.* Such is her commentary on self-pity "Self-pity in its early stage is as snug as a feather mattress' (*GT* 17). Her generalizations reflect her mature mind. Their reductionistic quality echoes the pithy maxims popularized by the French writer, La Rochefoucauld. They capture the attention of the reader by both content and form and are homey enough to make the reader comfortable.

The familiarity of proverbs, a folklore constituent, allows the message to be old or new, but purely palatable.

In *Gather Together*, Angelou takes special pains to expand on the complex personality of her mother Vivian and how influential she was on the development of Angelou's attitudes. This is a part of her metamorphosis from the child raised by Grandmother Henderson in narrow confines to the young woman capable of functioning in a larger world. Her mother is down-to-earth, practical, and, in keeping with tradition, is verbally proficient. Inspirational, she advises Maya that "Anything worth doing is worth doing well" (*GT* 81), and that Angelou should be the best at anything she can get into. Interestingly, she tells her, "Don't be a funky chippy. Go with class" (*GT* 84). Her mother cautions her to be on guard because "People will take advantage of you if you let them. Especially Negro women. Everybody, his brother and his dog, thinks he can walk a road in a colored woman's behind" (*GT* 108). Although her mother was kind, indulgent, and generous, she was not lenient nor was she permissive (*GT* 4). Her "capacity to enjoy herself was vast and her rages were legendary" (*GT* 105). Even though Vivian had made lots of money during World War II, she didn't accrue it without effort. She never wasted her time and studied to obtain diplomas in several areas to suit available employment: "barbering, cosmetology, ship-fitting, welding," etc. (*GT* 110). Her enthusiasm and energy are contagious. And Angelou is cast in the same spirit mold.

As for "Momma," Angelou finds her still "right-thinking" and still "slow-speaking" (*GT* 61) on her final visit to Stamps. To Momma, "Christ and the Church (are) the pillars of her life" (*GT* 64). To Angelou, these teachings are forever a part of her being, but are not the entirety of her life.

There is no kind word in the book for her father, Bailey
Johnson, Sr. She hates his "posturing and er'ering" (*GT*
144). But she does treat her brother Bailey, Jr. well. She
admires his quick mind and his eloquent voice and
dedicates *Gather Together* to him. He is a product of a
common background, one in which their father played no
part. Life went on in spite of Bailey, Sr.'s disinterest, and
his offspring made of themselves what they would.

Gather Together, although recognized as better written,
received less attention than the initial Angelou book, *Caged
Bird*. Many of the incidents in it are rather bizarre.
Whereas *Caged Bird* presents four anecdotes -- the
graduation ceremony, the boxing match, the breaking of
Mrs. Cullinan's china, and the trickster story of Red Leg --
acknowledged as genuine folklore. Many of the *Gather
Together* characters Angelou meets in her youthful travels
inhabit the demimonde, a world not to be admired.
Angelou rejects the alternatives explored in *Gather Together*
and keeps searching for a more rewarding life style. The
raffish content makes it difficult to accept *Gather Together*
as an exemplary literary effort, except for one very
important thing: style.

Angelou's knack for noting the similar in the dissimilar
-- for creating striking similes -- is again evident in *Gather
Together*: "looking like death eating a soda cracker" (*GT*
23) and "crazy as a road lizard" (*GT* 12). Angelou also
weaves in many vivid invented compounds in her narrative,
as she did in *Caged Bird*: "never-could-have-happened
land" (*GT* 63) and "flesh-real and swollen-belly poor" (*GT*
61). She continues to capture successfully the rhythm and
flavor of colloquial language as exemplified by Momma:
"You was downtown showing out." These constructions
never interfere with the reading of the book, but definitively
delineate realistic characters. The creative metaphors of

Angelou color every page. The critical consensus holds that these "poetic" language devices contribute to a readable and engaging narrative. They stand as evidence of her finely-tuned ear and her appreciation of the well-turned phrase. Angelou squeezes diverse comedy and humor from the anguish of the confrontations she experienced as a child and adolescent. *Gather Together* as well as Angelou's other narratives includes a share of scatological humor. This folksy form is easily understood by any audience. In *Gather Together*, profanity is fairly extensive, reflecting the tone of the times, post World War II, and the locus. "You're no shitty-ass baby" *GT* 89) and "like many weak people they wanted to milk the cow, at the same time denying the smell of bullshit" (*GT* 48, 49) are but a couple examples of this colorful language. Again Angelou prefers to be explicit rather than sanitizing and thus rendering less realistic the language. She expects her readers to understand the appropriateness. The overall tone in *Gather Together* avoids truculence. There is still an anger often expressed about whites in commentary that is astringent. But it is not vicious. The spirit and pace of the narrative leaves no time to be vindictive. There are too many worlds to conquer. Angelou is always moving on and maintaining a positive outlook.

Gather Together closes the door on explorations of questionable activities and brings Angelou to the point of desiring a respectable, normal home life for herself and her son. She reaches another maturity plateau. The advice of Vivian and Bailey, Jr., who ironically epitomize and embrace street smarts, turn Angelou's intentions toward wholesome activities. They keep her focused on her themes of survival with style, finding her true self, and admiration of literacy. *Gather Together* explores the perimeter of the cage but finds its focus in a continuity of purpose.

3. *Singin' and Swingin' and Gettin' Merry Like Christmas*
   "Climbing Jacob's Ladder"

Another bright, breezy title brings on book three of Maya Angelou's journey through life. Although the title is more or less self-explanatory, Angelou expands upon its derivation in an interview. The title comes, she says, from

> a time in the twenties and thirties when black people used to have rent parties. On Saturday night from around nine when they'd give these parties, through the next morning when they would go to church and have the Sunday meal, until early Sunday evening was the time when everyone was encouraged to sing and swing and get merry like Christmas so one would have some fuel with which to live the rest of the week.[39]

Many of the features of women's autobiography and of black autobiography canons are present in *Singin' and Swingin'* (1976). Angelou is now in her early twenties and many of her current concerns -- apprehension about her son, a desire for a home, facing racial conflicts, and seeking a career identify with the canons and appear in the beginning chapters. Facing a broader world populated with an increased number of whites, Maya re-examines her lingering prejudices and re-evaluates her relationships. This in-depth review of life in progress is often found in African-American narratives. As a traditional, structural device, it provides a point of retrospection from which changing views may be accomodated without guilt or explanation. It is a natural extension of growth and development. Interracial interaction can be better assessed individually in maturity.

The five years covered by *Singin' and Swingin'* include a wide geographical range, as has come to be expected in Angelou's books. She tells about going from a rather pedestrian life in San Francisco to a beginning night club career there that propelled her to New York, to Montreal, and then to Italy, France, Yugoslavia, Spain, Israel, and Egypt. She winds up in Hawaii, quietly contemplating her options as the book ends. She has circled back again to embrace motherhood and its importance to her life.

Angelou's attempts at re-entering the legitimate employment market found her working at a small real estate office and doubling at a dress shop to eke out a bare existence for herself and her son. She often visited a record shop run by a white woman, Louise Cox. Angelou still had trepidations regarding mingling with white people. Cox was impressed by Angelou's musical knowledge and offered her a job in the record shop. Angelou accepted with reservations but soon learned that her suspicions about the motives of the white Louise Cox were unfounded, and a genuine friendship ensues.

Angelou is seeking peace of soul and Cox encourages her to look at the Christian Science religion. Then the record store partner, David Rosenbaum, tells Angelou about a new rabbi at his temple and Angelou checks out this avenue of solace. Through Jewish religious music she finds many parallels with her own black heritage, but does not find the sense of belonging she seeks from either of these faiths. Her fear of death, precipitated by a concept of a frightening God in her native C.M.E. church, remains a major concern to her but she is still strongly attracted to her familiar music and prayer. Her faith is never lost.

At the record shop, Angelou meets a young, white seaman who shares an interest in her popular music. They

begin dating and the young man of Greek ancestry, Tosh
Angelos, soon proposes. Maya's mother had warned her
"that white folks had taken advantage of Black people for
centuries."[40] and was amazed that Angelou could even
consider marrying a white. But Tosh is a good man who
treats Angelou well and she is sufficiently attracted to him
to indeed marry him. He is a positive father figure for Guy
and an intellectual partner for Maya. Vivian had told her
that African-American women were not acceptable to their
community if they married a white man and surely not
welcomed by whites.   Angelou experiences negative
reactions to her and her husband: ". . . people stared,
nudged each other, and frowned when we . . . walked in the
parks or went to the movies" (*SS* 29). She felt guilty for
having a white husband; she had betrayed her race by
marrying one of the enemy. But whites should not believe
that she had forgotten the past. She often slipped out to
attend black church services and was still firmly tied to her
own religious roots. She wrestled constantly with Tosh's
expressed lack of faith. One day, Tosh exhibits anger
toward her and Guy and besides he is tired of marriage.
Just before the break-up of their short marriage, Angelou
expressses resentment of her recent treatment by Tosh in
black and white terms. She demands, "Who the hell was
he? A white-sheeted Grand Dragon of the Ku Klux Klan?
I wouldn't have a white man talk to me in that tone of
voice . . . . " (*SS* 36). After the divorce, although Tosh
leaves her with whatever little they had accumulated, she
complains bitterly that "Again a white man had taken a
Black woman's body and left her hopeless, helpless and
alone" (*SS* 38). This, Angelou's first marriage, became just
another adventure and betrayal.

   Angelou herself is the primary character of *Singin' and
Swingin'*. Her son Guy is the other person of prime

importance. Their individual and mutual growth,
development and diverse activities provide the movement in
the narrative. Momma -- Grandmother Henderson -- is
mentioned only briefly in this volume. She dies early in
this period while Angelou is hospitalized for an
appendectomy, and life moves on. Her immediate influence
is now negligible, but her early inculcation of Angelou is
always apparent. Quotes from Momma bind together all the
books. Brother Bailey is also a minor player in this part of
Angelou's life. He reinforces Maya's capabilities and offers
reassurance, but drifts away into pursuits of his own.
Mother Vivian Baxter exerts more influence as Angelou
moves toward greater independence. Her advice and
maxims, always adroit and pithy, are sprinkled throughout
the book and help Angelou function in her unfamiliar world
of choice. A best friend, Ivonne Broadnax, is a realist who
serves as a confidante and frequent advisor for Maya. She
provides stability of a sort. A large cast of people move
throughout the book, exerting a force and variety of actions
that propel Angelou ever forward. These strong, usually
successful people, black and white, help Angelou find a
degree of success and a self-assurance that carries her to yet
another level of achievement.

In this volume, Angelou takes her first step in a career
as a dancer and singer. Moving into the role of a
professional entertainer is a turning point in Angelou's life.
She now enters another layer of society: the creative world
of show business -- of singers, dancers, musicians, writers,
and producers. This is a group in which one's place is
determined by talent, not by color or riches or happenstance
of birth. As Angelou pursues her new career, she is often
invited to parties given by the chic, sophisticated, and
accomplished. Party, as alluded to in the title, seems to be
the canvas of this book. The folklore of old, so prominent

in the prior books, does not fit with the glitz of show business. Angelou goes to work at a small unknown club and soon acquires a local following. She is discovered by a performer of some note who is impressed and quite taken with the Angelou personality. Angelou's sense of humor and ingenuousness captivate the jaded sophisticates.

The first party of any importance in the story is one given by this chanteuse from the Purple Onion night club. The round of parties begins and this one is soon followed by a party on a boat owned by a painter who is part of an international San Francisco clique. Angelou becomes the current toy of this group and finds herself flattered and comfortable with the eclectic crowd. Much later, during the *Porgy and Bess* tour, there is a pre-Christmas party in a house in Yugoslavia reminiscent of the multi-national San Francisco gatherings. Each of these parties, by exposing Angelou to a progression of intelligent, keen, vital people, increases her self-esteem and sophistication. Each marks a step forward in her growth and acceptance of a world of differences and similarities. Each demonstrates her propensity for worldly knowledge.

The biggest party by far of the book is the ongoing party that Angelou recounts about a lively, energetic, loving, and talented group of sixty African Americans, including Angelou, who toured Europe and the Middle East performing the George Gershwin musical, *Porgy and Bess*. To call this tour a party is not stretching the term. The account of the antics of this entourage comprises the greater part of the book.

In every country Angelou visits on this tour -- and later on other trips she takes -- she buys a dictionary to help her learn the language of the country. She seeks out natives with whom she can practice speaking, and in a few years, she can proudly say that she is proficient in several

languages. Language facility seems to hold a special
meaning to Angelou and is often mentioned by her as a
point of achievement. It was once commonly held that
African-American singers could not handle the language
requirements for operatic roles. It took the tremendous
talent of such as Roland Hayes and Marian Anderson to
break the barrier against African-American concert singers.

As previously noted, in many women's
autobiographies the interest in career is usually given
secondary importance. But in *Singin' and Swingin'*
Angelou seems to balance evenly the relating and the
unfolding of her show business career with the recounting
of the tension generated when a black female tries to
function in a white dominated world of the 1950s. She
admits the consequent constant modification of her
perceptions of black-white relationships. A close reading of
the narrative of *Singin' and Swingin'* reveals over fifty
references to black ideas and attitudes about whites that
Angelou had absorbed from her background, from her
"Momma," and from her mother Vivian. This heavy
concentration on the black perception of whites rather than
the travel to exotic countries and the fun at parties is
primarily what makes *Singin' and Swingin'* worthy of
serious consideration. In expressing her perceptions,
Angelou continues to avoid the temptation to be polemic --
to be on a soap box. Instead, Angelou selects "engaging"
stories and in telling them uses these stories as vehicles to
weave in strong forceful statements that convey firmly her
indignation and ire about black displacement. But she is
ambivalent in her expressed feelings at the time covered by
this book. Yet, throughout this period, most of Angelou's
experiences with whites are positive.

Angelou recalls reeling with delight and disbelief when
the chic world of the Purple Onion night club accepted her

as a person. She confesses how immature her stance about whites had been: "My God. My world was spinning on its axis, and there was nothing to hold onto. Anger . . . and prejudice, my old back-up team would not serve me in this new predicament" (*SS* 74). Her ideas about Africans are also modified. When the boat carrying the *Porgy and Bess* cast approaches Alexandria, she is pleased to notice that the tall white buildings on the shore belied the old statement that "all Africans lived in trees like monkeys" (*SS* 200). So when she lands on shore, she fully expects to see kinsmen Africans that were "Tall and dark-brown-skinned. Proud and handsome like (her) father. Or Bitter-chocolate black like (her) brother" (*SS* 200). To her dismay, she finds the opposite is true. The first Africans she beheld did not at all look like her father, brother, or uncle. She is also distressed to see that the jobs in the hotel are distributed on the basis of color. The doormen and bus boys were black and brown and the hotel manager and bartenders were white. She saw many street beggars and realized that Egypt still had much work to do taking care of its poor. Her first glimpse of African shores shows no Utopia. Thus her arrival-joy is diluted, but it was not totally spoiled. While she sympathized with Egypt's economic problems, she learns pride in the fact that she is an American and finds herself drawn more positively toward home. This gives a glimpse of her future relations with Africa.

Like the two previous Angelou autobiographies, *Singin' and Swingin'* was received with generous criticism. Kathryn Robinson predicted quite accurately that "This latest segment in Angelou's continuing autobiography will be received with the same enthusiasm as earlier books . . . . Angelou continually succeeds in sharing her vitality, and *Singin' and Swingin'* should find a wide audience."[41] And Linda Kuehl finds that Maya Angelou continues to invent herself: "Maya Angelou is a self-conceived picaresque heroine.   She lives her life as though it were a story, which is one reason why it transcribes so naturally to the printed page."   Kuehl, however, prefers the "surging rhythm of *Caged Bird*, although *Singin' and Swingin'* is very professional, even-toned, and . . . quite engaging."[42]   R. E. Almeida also predicted quite accurately that,

> Most Angelou-philes will find (*Singin' and Swingin'*) a pleasant sequel . . . of this fascinating woman . . . . It is her perceptions of herself as a black, a woman, and a mother as well as her impressions of those she meets which distinguish this account. Her religious strength, personal courage, and her talent prevail.[43]

Singin' and Swingin' is labeled rather disappointing, however, by reviewer Margaret McFadden-Gerber, who feels it loses power by being more public and less introspective than the previous two volumes. In a time rife with political and social movements, the revelations of a strong, African-American female such as Angelou would have been sought out and welcomed, according to McFadden-Gerber.   Her observations and opinions would have greatly enhanced the book's importance.[44]   However, the reviewer appears to be judging Angelou's stature from a current point of view, not from where she was at the time embraced by the book. Angelou was still finding herself and evolving as a person. Her status at that particular time did not attach any significant political   importance to her utterances.

Angelou does briefly mention a discussion in which she defended the Brown vs. Board of Education Supreme Court decision of 1954 that declared separate but equal school systems unconstitutional.   Her single reference to the McCarthy virus which was weakening the body politic is in describing it as a "witch hunt" (*SS* 99). She does not, however, describe her inner thoughts on the usual range of topics, personal or public. Thus *Singin' and Swingin'* is less weighty than it might have been. The last hundred pages of *Singin' and Swingin'* consist of show business anecdotes that occurred in various places the *Porgy and Bess* company visits on its tour. Considering the age of the heroine and the exhilaration of her experiences, the tone of the book is appropriate. Its style is consistent with its predecessors and again depends heavily upon shared humor and light entertainment. The impact of the breadth of her exposures completes the youthful flings of Maya Angelou. The quiet ending re-affirming her responsibility as a parent marks yet another stage of maturity. The autobiographical sequence is naturally maintained. There is a proper use of words and pacing for the milieu of the adventures of this phase of Angelou's life. Her paragraphs find closure through appropriate proverbs and insights: "Avarice cripples virtue and lies in ambush for honesty" (*SS* 205).

Singin' and Swingin' is a journey of discovery and rebirth -- as a Black Christian, as Maya Angelou, and as a mother. It marks the emergence of Maya Angelou, a woman born of the childhood experiences and adolescent explorations of Marguerite Johnson and a woman whose talents have opened new doors and dictated new directions. This is also a woman upon whom the yoke of Motherhood has finally settled. The highs and lows of the journey have forged a stronger person more aware of human frailities and more attuned to her own. The quiet, positive ending leaves the audience anticipating the future conquests of Maya as she forges her way through life. She has once more affirmed survival, self-awareness, and devotion to learning as guideposts to living with style.

4. *The Heart of a Woman*
"Seeking Significance"

The title of Angelou's fourth autobiography, while less
striking or oblique than titles of her preceding books, is
taken from a poem by Georgia Douglas Johnson, a Harlem
Renaissance writer. This poem is marvelously appropriate
as it refers to a *Caged Bird*, thus providing linkage with
Angelou's initial series volume. This addition to the
ongoing story of Maya Angelou looks into the heart of the
maturing woman and focuses on relationships. The
relationships with her son, with men, with her racial
responsibilities, and with her writing are the thrust of the
narrative. These are the normal, everyday concerns, less
venturesome and startling. Racial confrontations such as
that of Angelou with white school authorities and that of
the renowned Billie Holiday versus a nondescript white
woman fulfill elements of the black canon of autobiography
and therefore discount any drift from the interest of her
people. Thus *The Heart of a Woman* (1981) is truly a story
of an African-American female. It does not depart much
from the factual happenings except for dramatic effect. It
is a far more sober assessment of her wide ranging
activities.

The Heart of a Woman does not disappoint the Angelou
readers who are accustomed to crisp, poetic prose
interspersed with "down home" homilies. It is another
professionally written work, exhibiting increasing literary
competence. The appellation "poetic temperament" holds as
true here as in her other books. The prose is captivating; it
maintains the richness and texture of her style. The
metaphors are still striking: "Time wrapped itself around

every word."[45]   Angelou continues to use scatology to capture individual speech practices. The essence of Billie Holiday cannot be captured without quoting her colorful, uncensored responses. Angelou is proud of Billie Holiday's friendship and would never demean it by scrubbing street-smart Billie's less than sanitary language. What you hear is what she is.

Angelou fictionalizes dialogue to re-create a sense of place and a sense of history. She incorporates fantasy to reveal her illusions and unfulfilled desires and to acknowledge her lack of control over the future. A degree of fatalism is woven throughout this and other Angelou works. There is a consistent acquiesence to fate. These rhetorical devices are commonly employed by autobiographers for realism and conviction, according to Carol E. Neubauer.[46]   Angelou does not stray far from traditional structure.

Critics responded favorably to the professional quality of *The Heart of a Woman.*   Janet B. Blundell calls it "lively, revealing, and worth the reading"; however, she saw a weakness in that it is at times "too chatty and anecdotal."[47]   But this is the very crux of Angelou's narratives.   They are generally a mosaic of episodes -- anecdotes -- linked by theme and character.   Sheree Crute seems to appreciate this approach and says Angelou "makes the most of her wonderfully unaffected story telling skills."[48]   *Choice* writes that "while (Angelou's) first book remains her best . . . every book since has been very much worth the reading and pondering."[49]   *Caged Bird* gains much of its strength from an extensive use of folklore, a significant omission in *The Heart of a Woman.*   However, this and other books since *Caged Bird* are less general in scope. The reviews of all Angelou's books are marked by a uniformity of light praise but great admiration. No critic suggests that any of the works in the series is less than a delight to read. The courage of the author's revelations is always applauded.

The Heart of a Woman, as *Singin' and Swingin'*, entails constant movement. Angelou is still seeking to find an appropriate home for herself and her son. This is made more difficult by her ongoing efforts to define herself. This is another volume covering a lot of geography and growth. Angelou moves from San Francisco to a Sausalito houseboat commune trying out the beatnik life style; thence to ultra conservative Laurel Canyon in Los Angeles. Lack of acceptance and racial attacks send her off to the Harlem Writers Guild in New York. She restlessly followed her fate to London to Egypt to Ghana, where the book ends. Whenever the opportunity presents itself, Angelou inserts her rich descriptive passages about these places visited. These descriptions enhance the specific experiences recalled as well as the general credibility of the narrative and also show an appreciation of the diversity of the world. This reflects Angelou's growing familiarity with an enlarging sphere and her comfort within it.

The Heart of a Woman picks up Angelou's story after she has left the cast of the European traveling company of *Porgy and Bess* and returned from Hawaii to the night club circuit in America. The book begins at the precise end of its predecessor. Angelou is still the unmarried African-American female with a rapidly growing now adolescent son to support. She is principally concerned during the seven years covered by *The Heart of a Woman* with her relationship with her son -- her love of him and her pride in his developing personality and character. Uppermost in her mind is his welfare and helping him cope as a black young man-child trying to mature in a generally unsympathetic white world. He has been taken care of on occasion by others, but Angelou continuously accepts motherhood and its attendant responsibility to monitor his development. This sense of duty incorporates a family relationship, and Angelou is concerned with establishing a complete family, which includes a father figure for Guy. This quest for family brings Angelou to describe her encounters with a number of lovers and potential fathers. In the time-frame of the book, she reports on relationships with several men, the last of which is her ill-fated common law marriage to her second "husband," Vusumzi Make, a colorful African radical. This is the liaison that carried her to London, Egypt and Ghana. She eventually finds Make to be a less than desirable role model for Guy and a trying mate for herself. They part after a few years.

A large portion of the book concerns involvement with the Civil Rights movement of the late 1950s and 1960s. Here, she seizes the opportunity to express her pride in her race and in its struggle for equality and acceptance. Like Norman Mailer in his *Armies in the Night*, Angelou serves as an informed personal historian of the moral crisis of the period -- racial injustice -- that was of popular concern. She is an enthusiastic participant in the movement and not just an outside observer. Daisy Aldan's previously quoted concern regarding the book's ". . . hostility . . . toward all white people"[50] is an outgrowth of the barrage of negative racial experiences Angelou relates. Every possible slur, slight, and affront is visited upon Angelou and her son solely because of their color. This emphasis also seems to be a justification of the motivations of the black activists who people the book. The more moderate views of Martin Luther King are reported too, and with great admiration. When Angelou chooses to work with an organized group, it is the Southern Leadership followers of Doctor King.

In the early books, Angelou's mother and grandmother

command a considerable amount of attention. Grandmother Henderson has died and is now rarely mentioned, but Angelou still calls on her mother when she needs reinforcement. Vivian provides her with pragmatic advice in the form of proverbs derived from Mother Wit: "Ask for what you want and be prepared to pay for what you get" (*HW* 29), a statement that encourages Angelou to be self-reliant and not to expect handouts. This and a lengthy Br'er Rabbit story are the few touches of folklore in *The Heart of a Woman*. This type of imbedded preachment covertly conveys its message.

Angelou accepts the demands of womanhood and is fiercely independent, but is grateful for her mother's support, be it financial or moral. This does not diminish her strength or independence, but rather increases them by knowing that there is a safety net in the person of Vivian Baxter. Angelou does take her son and move away from Vivian's immediate vigilance. Overcoming racial discrimination, she seeks greater independence and middle-class respectability in Laurel Canyon, Los Angeles.

Angelou's love of her son and involvement in his upbringing cause her to realize the special problems faced by African-American mothers when raising their children. Authority, she notes, is "in the hands of people who do not look or think like the (black mother) and her children. Teachers, doctors, sales clerks, librarians, policemen, welfare workers are white and exert control over her family's moods, conditions and personality" (*HW* 37). The African-American parent of that time is obliged to adhere to the existing and white societal coda. The red tape and restrictions may chafe as reported by Angelou, but they maintain order of sorts for all persons.

In spite of the problems articulated in *The Heart of a Woman*, Angelou succeeds in raising a son who turns out well. She does not fail him, and others in her position can thus hope for the same. One particular problem faced by single parent Angelou is that Guy has been hurt by the brief but frequent family separations. Having endured her own feelings of betrayal when passed to different relatives, Angelou knows she must compensate so Guy does not harbor resentment to her and turn to outsiders for guidance. She realizes how much Guy feels the need of a father. It was also painful for him to be a young man "who had lived with the certainty of white insolence and the unsureness of moving from school to school, coast to coast, and . . . made to find his way through another continent and new cultures" (*HW* 267). Therefore the determined search for family and father is so much a part of *The Heart of a Woman* that it cannot be isolated from the situational responses.

This search allows the introduction of a variety of male characters and allows Angelou to express normal sexual interests. This is an accepted topic of the culture of the time. Angelou reports on a series of lovers associated with her search for a suitable husband and father. Most fall short of her requirements. Angelou does try throughout the book to balance an honest appreciation of ordinary sexual adventures with the wholesome and desirable goal of stability. This is another message of hope for those young women disturbed by their sexuality and unable to come to terms with desires and expectations.

Angelou writes in this book much more graphically about her own sexual activities than in any of the preceding volumes. She is at an age and stage where this is natural and acceptable. One may tend to wonder how much of this detailed interest is real or romanticized. Her admission of shouting in the bedroom and such personal pleasure seems to be atypical material. In previous books, Angelou appears to contradict any extreme preoccupation with base pleasures. For example, in *Gather Together in My Name*, she imagines that the ideal husband made desultory love a few times and never asked for more and this was acceptable. In another instance, she said physical sex only once a month was satisfactory. Her stance was quite Victorian. This expectation may be closer to her real feelings than her "liberated" statements. Each of the contradictory positions may, however, merely reflect thinking of a particular time or circumstance. At the time of her writing *The Heart of a Woman*, more liberal and open talk of human interactions was developing. African-American female writers were not only taking pride in their race but also in themselves as women.[51] The "liberated" modern woman was free to proclaim that she too had sexual urges. Sometimes women seemed inclined to outdo each other for sheer shock value. Frank talk about sex seemed to be almost requisite for a commercially successful book of that era. Despite relating various affairs, Angelou always advocates monogamy and stresses fidelity in relationships. She honors commitment.

Angelou and Guy move from Los Angeles to New York. It was here that she met many of the men she discusses. Several friends had encouraged Angelou to pursue a writing career. She was accepted by the Harlem Writers Guild which was composed of black writers both neophyte and established. Angelou's work was roundly criticized, but the tough lessons provided needed direction. Her night club background supplied a living. Being in the cauldron of New York allows much of *The Heart of a Woman* to be devoted to the major and minor players of the Civil Rights movement and political activism of that period. Angelou's role as personal historian covers both the Civil Rights movement and the black literary movement. She meets and writes about such national figures as Bayard

Rustin, Malcolm X, Martin Luther King, and other prominent African Americans caught up in the push for equal treatment for their race. The inclusion of these prominent familiar figures allows for their lessons and messages to be passed along unobtrusively. When Angelou is a coordinator of the SCLC, she is totally involved in the cause. She is an excellent organizer and coordinates volunteer efforts, raises funds, keeps the office running, and attends innumerable functions with groups of various names. All this is for the purpose of furthering the advancement and recognition of black people throughout the world. She has been faulted by some for not being sufficiently involved in the "cause." This is not true; she just chose to be less strident. Her efforts were eminently successful, and her contributions to civil rights causes were effective. Together with Godfrey Cambridge she wrote and directed a well-received musical revue, *Cabaret for Freedom*, which was intended to raise funds and consciousness.

Angelou's sure ear allows her to re-create fictionally scenes of encounters with people with an uncanny touch of reality. She mimics dialogues with notable personages with ease. According to several informed friends, her descriptions of exchanges with Martin Luther King or Malcolm X capture the very essence of the responses they would give, although they are not quoted directly. Angelou is attuned to the intent of a message as well as its delivery.

Many Civil Rights advocates were not shy about acknowledging their African heritage. It is quite natural for them to mingle with and offer their support to Cuban and African Freedom Fighters. These foreign activists solicited assistance and appeared at many related functions. It is therefore not surprising that Maya Angelou aligns herself emotionally as a helpmate to one of these, Vusumzi Make, and fantasizes that together they can free all of Africa from white oppression. This is an unusual lapse from reality for Angelou. She is quite taken with Make and he steps into the role of the strong male she has been seeking. He relates well with Guy, relieving Angelou of sole concern. This largely influences her acceptance of him.

Throughout *The Heart of a Woman*, Angelou continues her indictment of the white power structure and her protests against racial injustice. She again re-creates scenes wherein the dialogue allows comment about shoddy white behavior. She sometimes utilizes flashbacks to youthful indignities endured and sometimes she relates experiences of friends and colleagues. The sketch of a scene involving Mother Vivian at the Desert Hotel in Fresno, California, is a classic. Vivian's every move and word is calculated to instruct Maya and deflate the ignorant whites they encounter. Vivian Baxter displays the ultimate in panache and carries off a put-down of her antagonists with dignity and distinction. Public negative treatment of African-American people validates their sometimes radical responses. The references to earlier affronts and reactions serve to provide continuity to the series.

Not all attitudes expressed regarding whites are negative. Angelou learns from Martin Luther King that he feels that there are many "white people who love right" (*HW* 94). Dr. King was optimistic. He had travelled to and from jails across the south and marched and preached throughout the United States, frequently with whites at his side or in his audience. He felt both white and black people were changing. Angelou herself was surprised by the white volunteers at the SCLC New York office. Although Angelou harbored a suspicion of white liberals, she was impressed by the honesty of actress Shelley Winters who ardently wanted only a peaceful future for her daughter in a mixed society. This idealism was somewhat misplaced; inequality and turmoil are extant today.

In relating experiences with whites, Angelou never offers solutions to the problems exposed. She simply reports, reacts, or dramatizes events. The closest she comes to an analysis or solution for racial problems is the time when she repeats Vivian Baxter's statement that "Black folks can't change because white folks won't change" (*HW* 29). Nevertheless the times were exciting and hopes ran high for progress toward equality.

Angelou's continuing role as a literary historian for the time of the book provides an opportunity to report on some African-American literature that is being published, despite her observation that it is difficult to get black literature accepted and printed. This is a somewhat inaccurate assessment, as many African-American writers were beginning to be published and publicized. Actually it was a time when book sales were in decline and all writers were encountering difficulties. There was a vast amount of publishable material and competition was keen. Talent, like seeping water, found someplace to go, and various movements enjoyed the efforts of the best and the brightest.

Vusumzi Make is called to London to present his cause and Angelou decides she will accompany him. She is committed to freedom for Africa and mixes with black women from many nations. The women did not actively participate in the conference but many exchanged ideas and objectives for their nation-states and people.

Make tells Angelou to find a New York apartment for himself, herself, and Guy. A family of sorts is born. They live well as befits a country's representative. Angelou keeps up her Harlem Writers Guild contacts and takes a leading role in Genet's *The Blacks*. Disturbing phone calls and events intrude upon the solidarity of the marriage, but

Angelou was pleased with Guy's progress. This outweighed all other things. They are suddenly evicted from their New York apartment. Angelou and Guy make a quick visit to Vivian in San Francisco while Make arranges to pack them off to Cairo.

For a time, the excitement of the exotic and the foreign mask the realities for Angelou. She soon finds, however, that Make is not faithful or truthful or capable of supporting them.

Initially in Cairo, Angelou is exposed to an increasingly sumptuous life style. But again, reality imposes, and mounting debts become burdensome. Work, to Angelou, becomes a necessity. A meeting with the president of a news service leads to employment for Angelou as an assistant editor for a new magazine, the *Arab Observer*. She avidly pursues knowledge of her new career and accepts her disillusionment with Make. Angelou took on additional work writing commentary for Radio Egypt. An inevitable breakup with Make left her heading to Ghana to enroll Guy in the university in Accra. She shakes off another betrayal by a man and is prepared to accept a job offer in Liberia and to loosen the ties with Guy and let each move along independently. Fate, in the form of an auto accident, intervened. Guy was seriously injured while with friends. Angelou was needed at his side and for a long recuperative period. Friends managed to get her a job at the University as an administrative assistant. She tends to Guy until he once again can function on his own. He moves into a university dormitory to finally begin his independent life. Angelou stays near to quietly launch this venture toward full manhood for her son. She is, however, contemplating following her own single personhood.

The Heart of a Woman follows Angelou's established pattern of ending on a strong note of hope. Angelou and her son Guy have advanced to the point where each of them can move toward divergent, independent paths. Angelou can relish a sense of achievement as Guy looks forward eagerly to his future. She can anticipate a future for herself centered on herself. Again closure brings the cycle to a place that portends a new life for both Guy and Maya, a re-birth: a closing door and an opening door. Both characters are now citizens of a large world. Faithful to the ongoing themes of survival, sense of self, and continuing education, *The Heart of a Woman* moves its central figures to a point of full personhood. Its light humor and bantering carries a message of achievement.

5. *All God's Children Need Traveling Shoes*
"Looking for a Home"

Angelou's two years in Ghana in the early 1960s provide the material for the fifth book in her continuing autobiography. The title, *All God's Children Need Traveling Shoes* (1986), is obviously derived from the popular spiritual, "All God's Chillun Got Wings." The clever reference to the ongoing search for place is couched in terms mindful of our ultimate home. Angelou's love of the spirituals of her African-American people, and her deep sense of religion is threaded throughout her works. Writing this when in her fifties, Angelou looks back on life situations of her thirties. Once again, the current autobiographical canons of a black woman writer are addressed in this book. Lynn Z. Bloom cites, "a radical transformation of American autobiographical canon, changing it . . . from an elitist group of works . . . by educated white men to literature much more representative of the American population, in gender, race, and class."[52] The focal point of *All God's Children* is Angelou the black, middle-class woman. She did not feel "threatened by racial hate"[53] while in Ghana and felt free to pursue her compelling desire to find her genesis.

All God's Children Need Traveling Shoes is another professional, rich, full, journeyman text. There is a polish of the writing in this book that exceeds her previous books. Her prose is often lyrical and soaring. Her literary accomplishments have resulted in an increased level of competency. She maintains her inventive metaphors and continues her personification of abstractions: "For me sleep was difficult that night. My bed was lumpy with anger and my pillow a rock of intemperate umbrage" (*AG* 142). She notes that Malcolm X also employs metaphors when commenting on racism in American life.

Angelou becomes introspective and deeply moved during reflective moments in this volume. Selections written about an African bridge, the castle walls of a slave prison and on the village of Dunkwa are all especially emotional. Angelou visualizes the chained masses imprisoned in the castle and hears the walls echo their cries. She reacts with great sadness and revulsion upon realizing the insidious involvement of brother tribesmen in the evil slave trade. Angelou is particularly moved by the inhumanity of the participants. She recounts another story of betrayal -- this time generic rather than strictly personal but an integral part of her heritage. It is easy to forget that slave trading was at one time an accepted normal business activity with deep historical precedents. It was never an American invention nor unique pursuit. However, it became ingrained in the new world and tolerated particularly blutal behavior and social indignities. America was slow to reject the practice.

The descriptive passages are true to Angelou's now well-developed style displaying vivid and captivating sentences and phrases. Both the content and the presentation lend themselves to quotable segments that lose no impact by standing alone: "These were the legions, sold by sisters, stolen by brothers, bought by strangers, enslaved by the greedy and betrayed by history" (*AG* 98). Frequently, this genocidal involvement of Africans in slave-trading is deliberately over-looked or misrepresented by black writers. Angelou has the courage to face the realities she discovers.

Angelou continues to sprinkle throughout the work amusing stories, jokes, and poems. Frequently the jokes indict whites, as has been customary in the previous four books. She is not yet ready to toss off the stings of prejudice, but tolerance and even a certain understanding can be glimpsed. She carefully balances her weighty insights with lighter sketches. The device of flashback is utilized on occasion, as customary to traditional autobiographical formula. It is of particular importance to tie this book to its predecessor. Angelou speaks somewhat more philosophically in this volume. She maintains continuity with her earlier books dredging up Mother Wit from her memory of early admonitions. She quotes one of her grandmother's perceptive observations, "If you want to know how important you are to the world, stick your finger in a pond and pull it out. Will the hole remain?" (*AG* 135). Biblical quotes are frequently incorporated into this text demonstrating that Angelou has not lost contact with her family roots even in the face of her broader search.

The first few pages of All God's Children repeat the closing events of *The Heart of a Woman*. This sets the scene and links the two books. As Guy moves to his own future he remarks to Angelou that perhaps she will now have her chance at growing up. This volume addresses that proposition. Angelou becomes totally involved in her search for a symbolic home and her admiration for Ghana. She revels in the vitality of the native and expatriate peoples she meets. She bonds with the landscape and the history of the country. Her ventures of inquiry produce moments of high emotion as she faces the places and people impacted by the earliest African slave activities. Her acceptance by natives and non-natives temporarily lulls Angelou into feeling that this thriving, progressive African state is indeed home. She eventually faces some of the weaknesses and flaws of being one with what is essentially a foreign land. The stirrings of ancestral humors do not replace the call of a homeland, however difficult that place may be. Finding the roots in Africa serve to further validate feelings for America. Although secure in having found the village and tribe from which she is descended, Angelou, according to Lynn Z. Bloom, will forever keep Africa and its welcome table within.[54] She has closed the circle of her quest for self by accepting that she is an American.

Once again, critics greeted *All God's Children Need Traveling Shoes* with generally kind remarks. Angelou was cited as "one of the geniuses of Afro-American serial autobiography."[55] The book makes "for absorbing reading,"[56] and her "prose sings."[57] She maintains a consistency in her writing that continues to charm and amuse her readers, and please her reviewers, most of whom are white. She thus demonstrates her broad appeal. In addition, *All God's Children Need Traveling Shoes* offers a reader "a wealth of information and penetrating impressions of the proud, optimistic new country of Ghana."[58] Angelou tested the entire manuscript on her close friend and valued confidante, Julian Mayfield, who was intimately acquainted with Ghana, having been a prominent expatriate at the time of her stay. He verified the book's accuracy. He only questioned details mentioned about an assassination attempt on Nkrumah. Otherwise, he approved and praised the content. Mayfield's acceptance and concurrence of her perceptions assured Angelou of the correctness of the text. Since so many of the people mentioned were still active and vulnerable, this was important. She had no wish to impact negatively on those who were working to develop a better world.

Julian Mayfield was close enough to Angelou, a brother figure, to write a fictionalized dramatization exploring an alleged relationship paralleling Angelou's affair with Vusumzi Make, which she details in *The Heart of a Woman*. His protagonists were thinly veiled replicas of Angelou and Make. This apparently did not draw condemnation from Angelou.

All God's Children Need Traveling Shoes, although a continuation of a chronological progression, can obviously stand alone as a separate entity for reading pleasure. Each volume of Angelou's autobiographical series is a well-written, entertaining addition to the literature of a race seeking just recognition for its accomplishments. Life as experienced by Angelou provides insights into what it means to be black and female in a variety of settings. Her wit and talent with words captivate a wide audience, crossing racial lines by virtue of pure entertainment.

The structure of *All God's Children Need Traveling Shoes* follows Angelou's pattern as an "anthology of anecdotes." A wide swatch of white space separates one incident -- one "chapter," as it were, from another; Angelou has dropped the practice in this book of numbering each segment traditionally. She is sufficiently mature and confidant in her writing to play about with form. Each

incident or section is autonomous, and therefore can be read
or analyzed individually and enjoyed without harm to the
text's coherence.   Two previously mentioned incidents in
All God's Children Need Traveling Shoes were reprinted in
popular magazines. The segment about travel in Dunkwa
appears in *MS* magazine (August 1986), and her eerie
experience related to the back-country bridge could be read
in *Essence* magazine (March 1986).   There is less
fictionalization and fantasy in this book than in the earlier
ones and its episodes lend themselves more readily to
independent quotation. The depth of observation in this
book's passages lends great credence to Angelou's
concentration on a search for self and home. Her responses
to the loci are penetrating and honest.   Her readers are
treated to unvarnished emotional insights.

The characterizations presented in *All God's Children
Need Traveling Shoes* move a step beyond the other
volumes in the series in that all of the familiar family
figures are no longer prominent. Other than Angelou and
Guy, the persons featured are new and old friends. Maya
Angelou attracts people to her as easily as the proverbial
flies to honey. Each of her books is populated with a wide
cross-section of the societies she encounters. She seems to
find warm supportive friends wherever she goes and meets
whoever of importance passes by. In the pages of this
book, these associations replace and supplant family,
indicative of greater independence.   She is indeed a
people-person and has come far from the mute, shy little
girl of Stamps, Arkansas. She is now caged only by her
own inclinations. Her winged adventures have given her a
worldly stage from which she can assess her life events.

Angelou departs from purely personal activities and
directs her attention to the Ghanian people. She admired
the Ghanian domestic and foreign politics and the persons

she encounters:

> Their skins were the colors of my childhood cravings:
> peanut butter, licorice, chocolate and caramel. I listened to
> men talk, and whether or not I understood their meaning,
> there was a melody . . .   (*AG* 20-21)

She feels a kinship mindful of her own real family.
The theme of racism has always been prominent in
Angelou's books. In this volume she opens her eyes to the
prejudice among various black groups and faces the
realization that racism is not the exclusive domain of
whites. She examines her own prejudices after a gathering
in Germany and modifies her perception. Malcolm X had
also recently concluded that there are whites he can call
brother. He said, Angelou paraphrases,

> that though his basic premise that the United States was a
> racist country held true, he no longer believed that all
> Whites were devils, nor that any human being was
> inherently cruel at birth. (*AG* 130)

All God's Children Need Traveling Shoes seems
quieter in tone than its preceding stories, although not
devoid of flareups. As mentioned, while placed in another
country, it contains a strong sense of home and a
rediscovery of homeland. The hospitality, the welcome, the
warmth, all contribute to a cocoon of belonging. There is
not the constant shifting from pillar to post and uncertainty
mandated by life's responsibilities in Angelou's other
books.   There is, as noted, much quiet reflection and
introspection. This is an ending -- to the dependent son
relationship, to exile, to blind prejudice, possibly to
Angelou's revelations. The quest is complete. Her circle
to herself is closed by the love she has shared in Ghana.

The pain of baring one's own soul has served its purpose. Maya Angelou emerges whole and in control. She discovers not only who she is, but where she belongs. But every sunset is followed by a new day, and every ending sets the stage for a new beginning. The faithful audience of Maya Angelou would no doubt welcome at any time another report on her new life in her old world. In the last dozen years, Angelou has seen considerable activity in diverse fields. She has written, acted, and pontificated on television and in personal appearances. Although her reading audience may be still waiting for more autobiography and amusing anecdotes, it would appear that this phase of presentation has lost its appeal to the writer. She has demonstrated stylish survival, she has found a comfortable self and home, and she is permanently a part of honored literati. Her themes have become her. There is no further need to write how it was. It is. Maya Angelou is widely sought as a person with current and future outlooks. She must have little time for looking backwards. Since her appearance at the President Clinton inauguration, she is in even greater demand as a speaker and pundit. Her humorous comments and insightful philosophizing are eagerly embraced and quoted. She frequents television and podiums across the country. The demands of the writing of books would be a drain on her energy, and after all - all God's children have walked all over God's heaven.

Notes

[1]Arthur E. Thomas, "Interview with Maya Angelou," *Like It Is. Arthur E. Thomas Interviews Leaders on Black America* (New York; Dutton, 1981) 6-7.

[2]Maya Angelou, *I Know Why the Caged Bird Sings* (New York: Random House, 1970) 230. Hereafter cited in the text as *CB*.

[3]Ernece B. Kelly, *Harvard Educational Review* Nov. 1970: 681.

[4]Kelly 682.

[5]E. M. Guiney, *Library Journal* 15 Mar. 1970: 1018.

[6]R. A. Gross, *Newsweek* 2 Mar. 1970: 90.

[7]Jeffrey M. Elliot, ed., *Conversations with Maya Angelou* (Jackson, MS: University Press of Mississippi) 151-52.

[8]Quoted in Marilyn B. Smith, "The Time of Their Lives. Teaching Autobiography to Senior Adults," *College English* 44, 7 (1982): 692.

[9]Gross 90.

[10]Elizabeth Schultz, "To Be Black and Blue: The Blues Genre in Black American Autobiography," *Kansas Quarterly* 7 (1975): 81-96.

[11]Schultz 85.

[12]Schultz 85.

[13]Schultz 86.

[14]Schultz 87.

[15]Schultz 91.

[16]Schultz 92.

[17]Schultz 93.

[18]Kelly 682.

[19]Francoise Lionnet-McCumber, "Autobiographical Tongues . . . ." Dissertation, University of Michigan, 1986: 74.

[20]Robert B. Stepto, *From Behind the Veil* (Urbana: University of Illinois Press, 1979) ix.

[21]George E. Kent, "Maya Angelou's *I Know Why the Caged Bird Sings* and Black Autobiographical Tradition," *Kansas Quarterly* 7, 3 (1975): 75.

[22]Lionnet-McCumber 74.

[23]Liliane K. Arensberg, "Death as Metaphor in *I Know Why the Caged Bird Sings*," *College Language Association Journal*, December 1976, 273-91.

[24]Stephanie A. Demetrakopoulos, "The Metaphysics of Matrilinealism in Women's Autobiography," *Women's Autobiography:*

Essays in Criticism ed. Estelle C. Jelinek (Bloomington: Indiana University Press, 1980), 180-205.

[25]Sondra O'Neale, "Reconstruction of the Composite Self: New Images of Black Women in Maya Angelou's Continuing Autobiography" *Black Women Writers 1950-1980.* ed. Mari Evans (New York: Anchor Books/ Doubleday, 1984).

[26]Demetrakopoulos 183.

[27]Phoebe Adams, *Atlantic* 233 (1974): 114.

[28]*Library Journal* 99 (1974): 1494.

[29]*Choice* 1 Sept. 1974: 920.

[30]Selwyn R. Cudjoe, "Maya Angelou and the Autobiographical Statement," *Black Women Writers 1950-1980.* ed. Mari Evans (New York: Anchor Books/ Doubleday, 1984) 20.

[31]Elliot 154.

[32]O'Neale 33.

[33]Elliot 154.

[34]Ruth Kanin, *Write the Story of Your Life* (New York: Dutton, 1971): 45.

[35]Carol Benson, "Out of the Cage and Still Singing," *Writer's Digest* Jan 1974: 19.

[36]Maya Angelou, *Gather Together in My Name* (New York: Random House, 1984) 3. Hereafter cited in the text as *GT.*

[37]Quoted in Cudjoe 8.

[38]Adams 114.

[39]Elliot 154-5.

[40]Maya Angelou, *Singin' and Swingin' and Gettin' Merry Like Christmas* (New York: Random House, 1977), 22. Hereafter cited in the text as *SS.*

[41]Kathryn Robinson, *School Library Journal* 23 Sept. 1976: 144.

[42]Linda Kuehl, *Saturday Review* 30 Oct. 1976: 46.

[43]R. E. Almeida, *Library Journal* 101 (1976): 1763.

[44]Margaret McFadden-Gerber, "*Singin' and Swingin' and Gettin' Merry Like Christmas,*" *Magill's Literary Annual* (Engelwood Cliffs, N.J.: Salem Press, 1977) 738-741.

[45]Maya Angelou, *The Heart of a Woman* (New York: Bantam Books, 1982), 9. Hereafter cited in the text as *HW.*

[46]Carol E. Neubauer, "Displacement and Autobiographical Style in Maya Angelou's *The Heart of a Woman,*" *Black American Literature Forum* 17 (1983): 123-129.

[47]Janet B. Blundell, *Library Journal* 106, October 1981, 1919.

[48]Sheree Crute, *MS* 10, July 1981, 27.

[49]*Choice* 19, January 1982, 621.

[50]Daisy Aldan, *World Literature Today* 56, 4 (Autumn, 1982): 697.

[51]Estelle C. Jelinek, *The Tradition of Women's Autobiography* (Boston: Twayne Publishers, 1986), 149.

[52]Lynn Z. Bloom and Ning Yu, "American Autobiography: The Changing Critical Canon," *Auto/Biography Studies* 9:2 (Fall 1994).

[53]Maya Angelou, *All God's Children Need Traveling Shoes* (New York: Random House, 1986), 29. Hereafter cited in the text as *AG*.

[54]Bloom and Yu.

[55]Houston A. Baker, Jr. *New York Times Book Review*, 22 May 1986, 14.

[56]Janet B. Blundell, *Library Journal* 111, 15 March 1986, 64.

[57]Jackie Gropman, *School Library Journal* 32, August 1986, 113.

[58]Gropman 113.

Chapter 4

Poetry: Something About Everything

Of Maya Angelou's six published volumes of poetry, the first four have been collected into one Bantam paperback volume, titled *Maya Angelou: Poems* (1986). Her early practice was to alternate a prose publication with a poetry volume, and a fifth "collection" follows her fifth autobiography. Unlike the four previous volumes of poetry, this fifth work titled *Now Sheba Sings the Song* (1987), adds a new dimension. Here fifteen or so short poems are responses to sketches of African-American women done by artist Tom Feelings, whom Angelou has known for many years. The combined talents of these two are highly complementary and the results are particularly appealing. A sixth volume, *I Shall Not Be Moved* (1990), contains new love poems and praise poems. A four poem inspirational collection has been available under the title *Phenomenal Woman*. These four are previously published poems.

Angelou's poems are a continuum of mood and emotion. They go from the excitement of love to outrage over racial injustice, from the pride of blackness and African heritage to suffered slurs. Angelou follows Countee Cullen's literary perspective that black authors have the prerogative to "do, write, create what we will, our only concern being that we

do it well and with all the power in us."[1] Angelou indeed
speaks out in many ways and with the best of words she
can summon.

Angelou's poetry is generally brief, in the tradition of
Langston Hughes who believed that a poem should be short
-- the shorter the better. Forty percent of the 135 poems in
the Bantam edition are 15 lines or less. Of this forty
percent, fifteen poems contain three stanzas, twelve have
two stanzas, and eleven poems are unstructured. These
eleven seem rather forced and rhetorical. Another dozen
poems contain between eleven and fifteen lines each. The
remainder of her 135 collected poems range from 30 to 50
lines. Angelou never indulges in lengthy narrative poems.
She chooses words frugally. The length of line in her
poems is also short. Most lines of her three-stanza poems
are trimeter; others, particularly those in the unstructured
poems, are from two to four syllables long. Some critics do
cite her poetry as "oversimplistic or slight because of the
short lines, easy diction, and heavy dependence on rhythm
and rhyme in her poetry."[2]   But Angelou herself has
frequently commented on the difficulty of reducing complex
thoughts and ideas to a poetic format. She says she begins
with many pages of words on her yellow legal pad and
works long and hard at distilling them.

Total poetic meaning stresses both emotional content and
rhythmical elements. If the emotional content can be
considered the bricks of the poem, the rhythm would be the
mortar that binds. Angelou is a natural builder of poetry
for she not only has a keen sensitivity to feeling, but also
a marvelous sense of rhythm. Her musical awareness is so
strong that she claims she *hears* music in ordinary, everyday
circumstances. A rhythmical awareness has been reinforced
by four important influences on her: first, her many
readings of the lyrical King James Bible;   second,

acknowledged reading of traditional white writers such as
Edgar Allan Poe, William Thackeray, and particularly
William Shakespeare; and of prominent black writers such
as Paul Laurence Dunbar, Langston Hughes, James Weldon
Johnson, Countee Cullen, and of W. E. B. DuBois' "Litany
at Atlanta." A third strong influence grew out of her
participation in the rhythmical shouting and singing in
African-American church services with their emotional
spirituals; and the strong, moving sermons preached in those
churches, whose tones she absorbed into her being. The
fourth shaping force derives from childhood chants, songs
and rhyme games long familiar in folklore, examples of
which are detailed in a prior chapter.

With her keen sense of feeling, it is natural for Angelou,
when she decides to compose a poem, first to find the
rhythm of a subject, however mundane that subject may
be. This approach is outlined in an interview with Arthur
Thomas as Angelou explains the lengthy procedure she
follows to produce a poem:

> When I write a poem I try to find a rhythm. First, if I
> wanted to write a poem about today. . . . I would write
> everything I know about today.
> Then I find the rhythm. Everything in the universe, Art,
> has rhythm. The sun rises and sets. The moon rises and
> sets. The tides come, they go out. Everything moves in
> rhythm. Tangentially, I would like to say that when people
> say of black people, "You have rhythm," it is not an insult
> . . . .
> It means that you are close to the universe. . . . I will
> find that maybe the rhythm changes. . . . This rhythm is
> slow and simple, and then maybe it's faster, more complex;
> and then there's the audience, and then -- it's marvelous!
> Exciting!
> *Then* I start to work on the poem, and I will *pull* and
> *push* it and *kick* it and *kiss* it, *hug* it, everything. Until

finally it reflects what this day has been.
    It costs me. It might take me three months to write that
poem. And it might end up being six lines.[3]

Angelou has often spoken about this painful process of
distilling her thoughts and the flow of her words. She
mentions that 15 pages of notes might end up producing
four lines of poetry. She has explained that the effort
involved encompasses a discipline that is very difficult. But
she finds the results rewarding and is still attracted to this
means of expression.

A few of her poems seem pretentious with somewhat
forced language, but most of her poetry has the spritely
diction of the vernacular and the dialectical. It is with this
language mode that she is most successful. She has no
objection to using dialect, as long as it does not denigrate.
She admires the dialect poems of Paul Laurence Dunbar
because of "the sweetness of them." The high regard for
this kind of poetry might have astonished Dunbar. He was
dismayed that his vernacular poems were more appreciated
than his romantic and cultured ones.

Of the poetry Angelou has published, only a few poems
first appeared in journals or literary reviews, the usual path
to publication for poets. Her work finds its way
immediately into books. R. P. Stepto waspishly observes
that Angelou's slight poems "cannot but make lessor-known
talents grieve all the more about how this thin stuff finds its
way to the rosters of a major New York house while their
stronger, more inventive lines seem to be relegated to the
low-budget (or no-budget) journals and presses."[4]
Angelou's 'thin stuff' is not so thin if read with an eye to
inner meaning. Her deliberate distillations are effective.
They are written for people, not other poets. Some of the
poems in her first volume, *Just Give Me a Cool Drink of*

Water 'fore I Diiie, were originally published as songs. The volume includes many of the lyrics from her 1969 recording of "The Poetry of Maya Angelou" for GWP Records. Most of her other poetry could easily be set to music. It is purposely lyrical. It is designed to elicit stirring emotional responses. Much of it is meant to show fun with the familiar.

There has been little critical attention given to Angelou's poetry beyond the usual book reviews. A scattering of negative responses have greeted each book of poetry. Ellen Lippman writes that " . . . Angelou is more adept at prose than verse . . . ."[5] Janet Blundell agrees: "This *Shaker, Why Don't You Sing?* poetry is no match for Angelou's prose writings."[6] A third reviewer, J. A. Avant, judges that " . . . this *Just Give Me a Cool Drink of Water* isn't accomplished, not by any means . . . ." But he concedes that ". . . some readers are going to love it."[7] And S. M. Gilbert suggests publishers have exploited Angelou. Gilbert comments that her second poetry book, *Oh, Pray My Wings Are Gonna Fit Well* ". . . is such a painfully untalented collection of poems that I can't think of any reason other than the Maya myth for it to be in print; it's impossible indeed."[8] It is not unusual to capitalize on a successful author's name. A new book by a currently popular writer generally guarantees at least minimum sales with minimum promotion. But Angelou had been writing poetry long before her prose ventures and has considered herself basically a poet. These negative reviewers have failed to look beyond the apparent simplistic lines to discover the power of their message. Angelou tries to reach readers not attuned to soaring poetics but comfortable with sparse exchanges.

Contrary to the negative criticism, positive comments have also appeared. The reviewer in *Choice* magazine finds that Angelou's work is ". . . craftsmanlike and powerful (though not great poetry)."[9] Chad Walsh says the work in *Just Give Me* is ". . . a moving blend of lyricism and harsh social observation."[10] The reviewer of *Shaker, Why Don't You Sing?* in *Publishers Weekly* says, her "poems speak with delicacy and depth of feeling."[11] Robert Loomis, Angelou's long-time editor at Random House, supports her with his well-taken remarks:

> I've always believed that those who have reservations about Angelou's poetry simply don't understand what she's doing. She is very strongly in a certain tradition of Black American poetry, and when I hear her read or declaim the works of other Black American poets, I can see very clearly what her heritage is and what her inspiration is. Furthermore, Maya is not writing the sort of poetry that most of us grew up in school admiring. What she is writing is poetry that is very definitely in what I would call the oral tradition. That is, what she writes can be read aloud and even acted. When her words are spoken, they are extremely effective and moving. They always sound just right.[12]

Although few critics have found great merit in her poetry, Angelou has acquired a dedicated audience. Her work seems to have a special appeal to college students. At her public readings, a generally balanced cross-section, male and female, black and white, is in attendance. She delights and enchants the entire group with her timing and her powerful delivery. Some admirers of her poetry have been so impressed with its rhymes, rhythms, and content that they themselves have been encouraged to write. Many poets manque have sent Angelou their unsolicited creations. Quite a few of these can be found stored with her collected papers at the Wake Forest University library. Angelou encourages young people to express themselves openly and seeks to inspire them.

The titles of Angelou's first four books of poems are attention getters. They are catchy black vernacular expressions. Her first volume, *Just Give Me A Cool Drink of Water* (1971), refers to Angelou's belief that "we as individuals . . . are still so innocent that we think if we asked our murderer just before he puts the final wrench upon the throat, 'Would you please give me a cool drink of water?' and he would do so. That's innocence. It's lovely."[13]

Angelou covers a wide range of subject matter. In Angelou's writings, poetry or prose, she holds to tradition and makes a special effort to dispel false impressions about African Americans, but does not use this as her sole motivation.

Angelou's poetry belongs in the category of "light" verse. Her poems are entertainments derived from personal experiences and fall into one of two broad subject areas. First, she writes about everyday considerations -- the telephone, aging, insomnia -- topics that are totally neutral. Second, she writes with deep feeling about a variety of racial themes and concerns.

"The Telephone," for example, exemplifies her universally identifiable reflections on an ordinary subject. She admits in verse that she is dependent on it. Its importance to her daily life is notable by a contrast to its periods of silence.

But she can't stand the quietude long, nor the isolation implied, and so she impatiently demands that the phone ring. This demand follows three structured stanzas: the first physically describes the telephone; the second, its active effect on people's lives; and the third, the effect of its silence. In the second stanza, she emphasizes the familiar and the feminine by employing a metaphor of sewing, tatting, crocheting, hemming, and darning. The intrinsic themes of black and blue and week-end loneliness are often found in popular blues songs. Another light general rumination is "On Reaching Forty." In somewhat stuffy language Angelou regrets the passage of time and expresses tongue-in-cheek admiration for those departing this world early and by this bestows upon the poem an unexpected conclusion. She is saddened by the passing of youthful milestones. The years forward will weigh even more heavily.

Inasmuch as Angelou is an accomplished cook, it is not surprising to find that she addresses the appreciation of traditional foods. In "The Health-Food Diner" exotic, faddish health food items are rejected in favor of standard fare such as red meat. In alternating tetrameter and trimeter quatrains, Angelou concludes each stanza with a food preference. Her reader finds life must be sustained by solid values, not notional influences.

Angelou not only has a keen ear for dialogue and dialect, but she also evidences a keen psychological understanding of an adolescent girl's romantic concerns and possessiveness. The speaker in "No Loser, No Weeper" expresses in the vernacular a universal sentiment. Again Angelou carefully structures her poem. In each stanza, the speaker notes how her reaction to losing something, beginning with childish items and advancing to that of major worth: in the first stanza, a dime; then a doll; then a watch; but especially in the last stanza when she truly hates to lose her boy friend.

The same subject matter -- the loss of a boy friend -- is expressed in "Poor Girl." The speaker is a teenager who addresses a fickle fellow playing the field. She's afraid there will be another disappointed girl in a long line of disappointed girls, just like her. One girl, she says, will believe the lies but can't be forewarned because of a possible misunderstanding. Eventually the truth will be realized and awareness will set in.

Angelou is a realist. She knows that a married man who sees other women usually returns home to his wife in spite of the attraction and charm of the Other Woman. The speaker in "They Went Home" is aware that she plays a loser's role. While the sentiment is psychologically sound, the lines are prosaic, reflecting the pitiful state of the abandoned.

Sometimes Angelou uses contrasting pairs in her poetry. For example, in "Phenomenal Woman," considered a personal theme-poem, she asserts the special qualities of a particular woman. The woman described is easily matched to the author herself. Angelou is an imposing woman -- at least six feet tall. She has a strong personality and a compelling presence as defined in the poem. One can accept the autobiographical details in this poem or extend the reading to infer that all women have qualities that attract attention. Angelou's dramatic presentation of this poem always pleases her audience and is frequently the highlight of her programs.

Angelou pairs this poem with "Men." The speaker is a woman whose experience has taught her the games men play. In this she uses a raw egg metaphor to contrast fragile femininity with dominant masculinity, but the female speaker has perhaps learned to be cautious.

Other contrasting poetic pairs are "America" and "Africa"; "Communication I" and "Communication II"; and "The Thirteens (Black and White)."

In *Gather Together in My Name*, Angelou describes being shown a room full of dope addicts and the impact this picture had on her. In both "A Letter to An Aspiring Junkie" and in "Junkie Monkey Reel" she details the dangerous consequences of using drugs. In both poems the slave master of today is drugs, and the junkie is tied to the habit as if he were the monkey attached to the street vendor's strap. Both poems contain particularly disturbing images.

Angelou uses every opportunity to build African-American pride and in "Ain't That Bad?" she praises black culture, mores, customs, and leaders. Its short lines, its repetition of imperatives, and its repetition of the title help constitute a chant, which categorizes it as a "shouting poem."

In black West African English (Sierra Leone) *i gud baad* means "it's very good." Thus "bad" as used extensively in this poem carries a favorable connotation, meaning to be "very good, extremely good." This meaning has been incorporated into everyday black vernacular and therefore is commonly understood. The last word in the last line of the poem sustains the positive connotations and provides a closure.

As detailed in an earlier chapter, a number of children's activities and responses have been handed down through the years in all cultures and are considered folk materials and light entertainments. This wealth of rhyming folklore, so important in Angelou's childhood, provides an indigenous and unconscious source of much of the style and the flow of both her poetry and prose. It dictates the structure of much of her poetry.

Angelou's second group of meditations is concerned with racial subjects and themes. This group allies poetry with morality by continuing the themes of protest and survival found in her autobiographies. These poems are not excessively polemical; they voice only mild protest.

In this category is Angelou's favorite poem and theme, "Still I Rise," the same title as that of a play she wrote in

1976. The title, Angelou says, refers "to the indominable spirit of the black people." She often quotes this poem in interviews and includes it in public readings. The poem follows Angelou's customary fashion of incremental repetition, and catalogues injustices.

In spite of adversity, dire conditions and circumstances; in spite of racial epithets, scorn, and hostility, Angelou expresses unshakeable faith that one will overcome; one will triumph; one will Rise! The lines remind us of the black spiritual "Rise and Shine" as well as other religious hymns that express hope: "Oh, rise and shine, and give God the glory, glory!/Rise and shine, and give God the glory, glory!" In "Our Grandmothers" Angelou voices a similar sentiment contained in another dearly loved spiritual: "Like a tree, down by the riverside, I shall not be moved."

The "I" in "Still I Rise' is designated female by Angelou herself as she numbers this poem as one of the four about women in *Phenomenal Woman*. She speaks not only for herself but also for her gender and race. This extension of self occurs in Angelou's autobiographies and protest poetry. It is in keeping with a traditional practice of black writers to personalize their common racial experiences. Moreover, Angelou implies that the black race will not just endure, but that in the words of Sondra O'Neale, "will triumph with a will of collective consciousness that Western experience cannot extinguish."[14] Angelou's most militant poems are contained in the second section of her first volume of poetry, "Just Before the World Ends." They have "more bite -- the anguished and often sardonic expression of a black in a white dominated world," Chad Walsh observes.[15] In her moving address "To a Freedom Fighter," Angelou again as a spokesperson for all blacks acknowledges a debt owed to those who fought earlier civil rights battles. They did more than survive; they endured all indignities for the maintenance of their race.

In "Elegy," the speakers are early black activists, Harriet Tubman and Frederick Douglass, who proudly observe successors to their cause, the torch bearers they spawned. In their battles for status, African Americans have experienced disappointment with political and social liberals. In her early twenties, Angelou wrote "On Working White Liberals," which expressed the prevailing cynical view of their broken promises. Liberal words have often been empty words, and so the black came to doubt their sincerity. The poem challenges white liberals to an extreme action to prove their racial tolerance. Words are not enough. Angelou has since disavowed the poem's sentiments; she says she was a young "hot-head" at the time she wrote it.

Angelou comes to the defense of Uncle Toms, people censured by black activists because they do not overtly resist unfair treatment. In "When I Think About Myself," Angelou explains why a black woman responds with a simple "Yes, ma'am" for the sake of a job, even to a young white who insults her with the offensive word "girl." The servant does not pity herself and knows she is keeping her race alive. By being servile for an entire lifetime, she has provided sustenance for another generation who may find better conditions. Whenever appropriate, Angelou voices approval of those who endured indignities to feed, shelter, clothe, and educate the family.

Angelou also praises the black slaves who helped build America. In "To a Husband," she reminds readers of this, and that the black man proudly reflects his African roots, while contributing to the physical growth of this country.

Angelou also idealizes black men and enhances their pride in her love poems. Two poems in particular in the

first section of *Just Give Me* present admirable images of
black men -- their color: Black Golden Amber; and their
behavior -- gentle and grave. In "A Zorro Man" love is
found to be exciting; the speaker is delighted that her man
is courageous and thrilled with her. "To a Man" admires a
man's special qualities: he is Southern, gentle, and always
changing. That Angelou dedicated her first book of poems
to Amber Sam and the Zorro Man is not at all surprising.
Her best poem in the section on love is "The Mothering
Blackness." In incremental repetition and with biblical
allusions, the speaker observes that black mothers forgive
their prodigal children. A black mother loves her children
simply because they are her children. These mothers refrain
from condemning and warmly welcome their wanderers.
Angelou's poem praises such unconditional love. Whenever
Angelou found herself troubled, she went home to her
mother or grandmother for nurturing; the bond between
them was always strong and supportive. It is a natural
consequence of motherhood in Angelou's mind.

Angelou speaks positively about women in various
mundane settings. "Woman Work" reinforces the saying that
"women's work is never done." It's a list of the endless
daily chores faced by a housewife and mother. Its lines do
not explain or complain. They merely list.

In "Momma Welfare Roll," Angelou tells how brave a
mother is when she accepts welfare. Circumstances force
survival to depend upon government largesse, but pride
dictates an attitude toward it. This poem acknowledges the
demeaning turmoil endured when accepting welfare
benefits. Malcolm X blamed his mother's death on the
bureaucratic bungling of social workers.

Angelou's poems are dramatic and lyrical. Her style is
open, direct, unambiguous, and conversational. The diction
is plain but sometimes the metaphors are quite striking.

The most successful of her poems are those that "have language close to speech or more nearly song,"[16] those written in the vernacular. When she steps outside this level of language, the resulting effort appears affected. An example is "Unmeasured Tempo." In this poem we find awkward, forced lines. Some of Angelou's best "poetry" might well be her song lyrics such as "They Went Home." When Paul Laurence Dunbar complained that his vernacular poems were better received than his romantic, he was referring to vernacular as the everyday language of the street as opposed to dialect -- that is, the black dialect of the "comic minstrel" tradition. The phonology of "yo" for "your" and the grammar of "be's" for "is" or of the zero copula are examples.

The use of the vernacular can convey a maturity, while the dialectical can imply a childishness, an inferiority. Angelou avoids anything that might make her race an object of ridicule, and the use of black dialect -- or soul talk -- might compromise dignity. Therefore, she chooses a language level perceived to be more dignified.

Angelou's poems read easily and smoothly by utilizing both rhyme and repetition, particularly incremental repetition. However, out of 39 poems in *Just Give Me* she uses rhyme in only seven and the rhymes she chooses are rather ordinary and unimaginative: approaches/coaches; weaving/leaving; or in another volume, cake with steak. She shows a keen ear for sound as when in "Harlem Hopscotch" she rhymes the words "left" and "hisself." There is also an occasional internal rhyme such as "Carrot straw" and "spinach raw" in "The Health-Food Diner."

Her theatrical sense exemplifies itself in her rhythms. In an interview with Bill Moyers on National Educational Television where they discussed black writers and white critics, Angelou said,

> Quite often there are allusions made in black American writing, there are rhythms set in the writing and counter-rhythms that mean a great deal to blacks. A white American can come in and he will hear, he will understand hopefully, the gist. And that's what one is talking about. The other is sort of "in" talk.[17]

As the fundamental appeals in poetry are the emotion, the feeling, and the rhythm, anyone can appreciate them in a successful poem, even poetry of different cultures. The "in" talk, on the other hand, refers to "signifying" wherein certain phrases evoke a response from an African- American reader but might be unknown to other readers. For example, the phrase "cigar-box guitar" means a string instrument associated with the devil but that most consider merely a primitive musical device. There are also words in black linguistic lore that have restricted meanings such as the word "dichty" in "Weekend Glory," which means "snooty," "high-hat," or "snobbishness." Line six in "Harlem Hopscotch" recalls a popular jingle of black origin:

> If you're white, all right
> If you're brown, hang around
> If you're black stand back.

A knowledge of black linguistic regionalisms and folklore enhances the appreciation of Angelou's poems. Thus a Whorfian "linguistic relativity" in which language shapes the way we view the world may be at work here. But most of Angelou's poems can be understood and appreciated on their own merits, sans special insight. Her topics of simple universal concerns embrace the breadth of everyday worldly encounters, and, through poetic presentation, uplift these ordinary experiences to special status for the ordinary reader.

The tone in many of Angelou's poems is somewhat muted and reserved. There is frequently a melancholy, a blues feeling. There are no explosive outbursts like John Donne's "Batter My Heart, Three Personed God" or "For God's Sake, Hold your Tongue"; nor outrage as in John Milton's "On the Massacre at Piedmont." Perhaps her restraint derives from the African-American attitude of fatalism which has been noted by many scholars and particularly evidenced in black folklore. Perhaps it is merely for the emphasis related to a mutual response.

The sound should echo the sense, as Alexander Pope suggested, and Angelou does achieve a correspondence of sound and sense in many of her poems. The monotonous rhythms and diction of her poem "Greyday" seem to echo the feeling of loss and emptiness without the presence of a loved one. The lines clearly depict the perception of a time of loneliness.

R. B. Stepto points out parallels between Angelou's poetry and that of Sterling Brown, Langston Hughes, and Gwendolyn Brooks, particularly "Annie Allen" and "the Bean-Eaters" of Brooks' pre-Black aesthetic period. He also notes Angelou's marriage of "work song" refrains and "protest" couplets and wishes she had developed this further.[18] In Angelou's latest collection, *I Shall Not Be Moved*, she does give testimony to hard work in the poem, "Worker's Song." This poem sings the praises of those whose work contributes to the orderly function of vital activities. African Americans do have a long history of hard work. In Angelou's writings, rarely is there anyone who does not work. Everyone of her characters -- singers, dancers, railroad workers, etc.-- works hard.

While Angelou's poetry is not generally acclaimed as great poetry, it is nevertheless highly enjoyable as J. A. Avant observes. Angelou may rank as a poet of moderate ability, but her poetry is praised for its honesty and for a moving sense of dignity. Angelou is consistently understandable, enlightening, and entertaining. Her personal readings of her poetry are moving events and greeted with great enthusiasm. Angelou plays an audience masterfully and her delivery enhances the most simple rhyme. It is little wonder she inspires novices; she makes the difficult seem simple and touching. This in itself is an accomplishment reflecting more than moderate ability.

Angelou discussed her crowning moment as a poet with Oprah Winfrey on a recent television interview. A telephone call came from Harry Thomason shortly after Bill Clinton's election as president. Clinton had asked to have Maya Angelou compose a special poem to be read, by her, at his inauguration. Angelou said she was overwhelmed, but went to work. She rented a hotel room, as is her practice when composing, took her pads and pencils and closeted herself from early morning to afternoon. She first settled on her theme, America, and then wrote down everything she could think of about the country. Those thoughts were then pushed and squeezed into a poetic form. The resultant poem, "On the Pulse of the Morning," was read by Maya Angelou from the ceremonial balcony at President Clinton's swearing in. Angelou herself does not consider it a great poem. She says it is a good public poem and carries the message of unity she intended. She has a frequently recurring theme that, as people of diversity, we are more alike than unalike. This idea is contained in the inaugural poem. Angelou feels that one day she will rework this material into a more important private poem. This distinction she draws between public and private poetry is worthy of note.

The notoriety attendant upon being only the second poet, and the first African American and first female, asked to be a part of such an important public event, has spilled into Angelou's life of quietude at Wake Forest University and put her again high on the demand list for public speakers. It also has led to renewed interest in her books and poetry and should result in greater academic evaluation of her lifetime accomplishments.

Angelou again went public with a specially written poem, "A Brave and Startling Truth," for the San Francisco celebration of the 50th birthday of the United Nations. She once more violated her stated belief that "'public' and 'poem' go together like buttermilk and champagne." She prefers her poetry to be a private experience, but answers when called upon if the cause is noble. The African-American Million Man March in Washington, D. C. in October 1995 was another request for a specially tailored tribute. She could not refuse her brothers and agreed to read on their program.

Maya Angelou has served her people well and has informed and entertained untold numbers of us. Hopefully, she will continue to do so and to point out our "alikes" and oneness.

Notes

[1]Countee Cullen, *Color* (New York: Arno Press, 1969) vi.

[2]"Maya Angelou." *Contemporary Literary Criticism* 35 (Detroit: Gale, 1985) 29.

[3]Arthur E. Thomas, *Like It Is. Arthur E. Thomas Interviews Leaders on Black America* (New York: Dutton, 1981) 5.

[4]R. B. Stepto, "The Phenonmenal Woman and the Severed Daughter," *Parnassus: Poetry in Review* 8, 1 (Fall/Winter 1979) 313-15.

[5]Ellen Lippman, *School Library Journal* 25 (1978): 83.

[6]Janet Blundell, *Library Journal* 108 (1983): 746.

[7]J. A. Avant, *Library Journal* 96 (1971): 3329.

[8]S. M. Gilbert, *Poetry* (August 1976): 128-129.

[9]*Choice* 9 (1972): 210.

[10]Chad Walsh, *Book World* 9 (1972): 12.

[11]*Publishers Weekly* 11 Feb. 1983: 59.

[12]Robert Loomis, "Letter to L. B. Hagen," 3 June 1988.

[13]Jeffrey M. Elliot, ed., *Conversations with Maya Angelou* (Jackson, MS: University Press of Mississippi, 1989) 155.

[14]Sondra O'Neale, "Reconstruction of the Composite Self: New Images of Black Women in Maya Angelou's Continuing Autobiography," *Black Women Writers 1950-1980*, ed. Mari Evans (New York: Anchor Books/Doubleday, 1984) 28.

[15]Walsh 12.

[16]Blundell 1640.

[17]"Maya Angelou," *Current Biography* (New York: H. W. Wilson, 1974) 14.

[18]Stepto 313-315.

Chapter 5

Films, Plays, Television, Essays: "Performer, Producer, Playwright"

Angelou's total creative productivity is marked by its diversity. It was once wittily noted that she has touched more bases than Hank Aaron. Angelou has worked in at least five forms with a fair amount of success: poetry, prose, film, stage, and television. Her prose autobiographies are generally regarded as the most successful of her literary endeavors. This is perhaps because her forte lies in embellishing familiar stories. The subject matter she handles in the five forms is strikingly similar: the themes of racism, relationships, and African-American heritage. While each literary form dictates a different presentation, the message and content need not differ. What is told in a lyrical poem can be dramatized in prose. Angelou apparently enjoys the forays into various genres and exhibits competent craftsmanship whenever she takes up her pen.

When Angelou won national literary recognition as a consequence of the stunning reception of *I Know Why the Caged Bird Sings*, 1970 became a benchmark year. Although her time before the publication of *Caged Bird* were years in which she was involved in many creative activities, the subsequent endeavors were limited by the demands of *Caged Bird's* sequels.

When Angelou was earning a living as a dancer and singer, she published her first short story in the magazine *Revolucion*. "That it would appear only in Cuba, and probably in Spanish, did not dilute the fact that I was joining the elite group of published writers." (*HW* 85). The Cuban communists courted African Americans and often provided a pulpit for their works. During that time she also wrote a number of clever, original songs for her night club routines. Many of these were later incorporated into her books of poetry and recorded for Liberty Records (1957) and for GWP Records, 1969. Along the way, Angelou acted in and composed two songs for the movie, "For Love of Ivy." Whenever asked, she would come up with something appealing and appropriate. Here again the challenge was always welcomed and met.

While still performing in California clubs in the mid 1950s, Angelou's writing ambitions led her to move to New York and join the Harlem Writers Guild, as has been mentioned. Members of the Guild were both brutally critical of each other and still supportive. They tested the mettle of their fellows but encouraged continuous production. Thus like many fledgling writers, Angelou had her fair share of unproduced and unpublished efforts. She admits to a tucked away novel that never was published and an unproduced play, "Getting Up Stayed on My Mind." Additionally, she wrote a two-act drama, "The Clawing Within" (1966) and a two-act musical "Adjoe Amissa" (1967), both unproduced. She also has a 1970s unproduced Hollywood script. After *Caged Bird* became a success, Columbia Pictures invited Angelou to Hollywood to be the fourth writer to attempt a script from Alex Haley's *The*

Autobiography of Malcolm X.[1]   Her script became just another in a long line of discards commissioned for movies but never filmed.   Many years passed before Spike Lee brought such a film to theatres.   Each experience added to her store of information and learning so nothing was ever a total loss.

Angelou's seemingly limitless energy and unbounded curiosity caused her to respond to whatever requests came her way.   Her background as a singer and dancer helped Angelou make an easy transition to acting.   She performed in a number of plays.   In 1954-5 she was "premier dancer" in the U. S. Department of State's European tour of Gershwin's *Porgy and Bess*.   In 1957 she was in *Calypso Heatwave*, an off-Broadway production.   She later wrote the songs for a movie also called *Calypso Heatwave*, starring the popular singer, Johnny Desmond.   In Genet's *The Blacks* (1960), Angelou played the White Queen in its off-Broadway production.   She also wrote music for this, but a payment dispute ensued.   This prompted her to leave the cast.   The thrust of *The Blacks* is that if power roles were reversed from whites to blacks, blacks would behave in the same fashion as whites.   Angelou reprised her role in the revival of *The Blacks* in Berlin and Venice.   Ironically, this play parallels Angelou's theme of "people are more alike than unalike."

Angelou found herself cast in roles in *Cabaret for Freedom* in New York in 1960; *Mother Courage* in Accra, Ghana in 1964; *Medea*, Hollywood 1966; and in 1973 she made her Broadway debut in *Look Away*, which resulted in a Tony nomination for the best supporting actor.   In 1977 she agreed to play Kunta Kinte's grandmother, Nyo Boto, in Alex Haley's television mini-series, *Roots*, in return for the chance to direct two segments of the series.   She received another Tony nomination for this supporting role.

Angelou has been seen in a variety of big and small screen parts. She played the role of a poetry professor in the 1995 television show *Touched by an Angel*, and appears in the movie *How to Make an American Quilt* with Winona Ryder and Alfre Woodard. Acting is an additional conquest for Maya Angelou. She apparently takes to it naturally and the accolades recognize her raw talent.

When involved in fund raising for the SCLC (Southern Christian Leadership Conference), Angelou, in collaboration with Godfrey Cambridge, wrote a highly praised revue, *Cabaret for Freedom* (1960). Credentials gained from this provided other opportunities. Subsequently she wrote and produced a play, *The Least of These* (1966). In 1974, she adapted Sophocle's *Ajax* for the modern stage. She explained the rationale for her approach in *Ajax*. She began to look for modern-day likenesses to *Ajax*. These were heroes who were allowed to die without due recognition beyond some retroactive applause.[2]

In 1973, Angelou had returned to her musical talents, writing and directing *And Still I Rise*, a dramatic historical indictment of racism which incorporated some of her poetry set to her music.

In 1983 GM productions backed the world premier of an Angelou play, *On a Southern Journey*. Nothing remains about its reception. Angelou makes reference in an interview to another 1983 one-act play, *Theatrical Vignette* but no review of this could be found.

Interspersing stage with film work, Angelou's screenplay, *Georgia, Georgia* (1972) for Independent-Cinerama, made her the first African-American woman to have an original script produced. She also wrote its musical score. The film centers around a black, internationally renowned pop singer who goes to Sweden to give a concert, falls in love with a white photographer, and is murdered by a racial zealot.

Black men, mainly a group of American defectors living in Sweden, are portrayed as exploiters. It is unusual for Angelou to present black men in a negative role. In the production of the film, Angelou had trouble with the director. She has stated that he was a European white male who was never in touch with the screenplay, no matter how she tried to reach him.[3] The orchestra director was also difficult. He did not allow her to do what she wanted with her own music. Peter Bailey of *Ebony* magazine devotes a lengthy review to *Georgia, Georgia*, and finds that Angelou, perhaps because of incompetence of the white directors, did not quite achieve her stated goal of showing black women as real people. Angelou is quoted as saying, "The black American woman has never been described in American letters."[4] Angelou puts Georgia in the throes of a black woman suffering from the psychological problem of "white fever." The singer and her homosexual manager are both caught up in being able to respond emotionally only to whites. The hired mother figure/companion portrays the traditional black counter stance and struggles to bring Georgia back into the flock. Her efforts are to no avail and her despair leads to the death of Georgia. This is potent material. However, reviewer A. H. Weiler finds its treatment too simplistic.[5] The white-hating maid versus the white-loving singer should provide more memorable scenes, particularly because of their basic need for each other. Another lengthy review praises Angelou for attemting to touch on areas rare for film, but finds *Georgia, Georgia* comes up short with the characters not fully developed.[6]

After the film was finished, Angelou returned to Sweden and took a course in cinematography. She reported that she wished to direct films and needed to understand the mechanics of the process and the workings of a camera to do this properly.[7] Angelou kept active in films. She became one of the earliest female members of the Directors Guild, and later wrote a screenplay for a little short film, *All Day Long* (1974).

In 1979, *I Know Why the Caged Bird Sings* was shown as a CBS special; Leonora Thuna was co-writer with Angelou. Michael Arlen in *The New Yorker* says they captured "the essence of the story in the television adaptation."[8] Earlier in negotiations for producing the play, Angelou as author had refused to let a young white man write the script and interpret on the screen the memories of her black-girl youth. Maintaining control of content was important to projecting that essence, Arlen noted. A review in Donald Bogle's book of Black American Film and Television productions feels the script comes up short when compared to the splendily written sensitive book. The article points out that the poetry and insights are not dramatized in the television work. It is found to lack the conviction and heroism of the book, and moves somberly without showing the development of the soul of a remarkable woman. A good cast seems to be hampered by poor direction. Nonetheless the airing attracted a large, satisfied audience.[9]

Angelou has worked extensively in television: she wrote, produced, and hosted "Blacks, Blues, Black "(1968), a ten-part series on African traditions in American life for National Educational Television. She served as a guest interviewer in *Assignment America* (1975). In 1976 she wrote two African-American television documentary specials, "the Legacy," and "The Inheritors." In 1977 she won the Golden Eagle Award for her PBS documentary, "Afro-Americans in the Arts." Another of her television credits is the PBS study course called "Humanities Through the Arts."

In 1979 NBC committed itself to a commercial series

pilot called "Sister, Sister," which Angelou conceived. The pilot sat on the network's shelf for three years before airing to critical acclaim in 1982. Bogle calls "Sister, Sister" a rarity of its time on American television. It is a look at the complicated lives of three black sisters trying to come to terms with themselves and with each other. The three daughters are drawn together in North Carolina by the death of their unremarkable, unlikeable father, whom the older sister had cared for over the years. She also was surrogate mother for the youngest girl who rather typically teenage dreams of being a professional ice skater and experiences first love. The wild, big city middle sister brings back with her a young son and ideas of freedom, rage, hostility, and a loose life. Angelou's script is faulted for going into too many directions and suffering from weak construction. There is an exuberant style and energy, however, that commands the audience follow the emotional dynamo and even enjoy being wrung out. The casting is remarkably apt and carries the characters to limitless highs. They seem to overcome the script's uneven movement and provide a production fascinating to a black audience, both by its familiar caricatures and content thrust. It is cited as one of the few shows concentrating on problems peculiar to black women to be aired.[10] "Sister, Sister" as originally presented did not find a scheduling niche and was not continued. Its commercial value may have been affected by timing. The thesis has recently been revived for another treatment. But this show too must not have found an audience as it was soon cancelled.

Angelou has been primarily associated with public television which is constantly a victim of funding shortages. Many worthy productions never reach an audience. Angelou has been fortunate to have had so much of her work actually presented. This is a tribute to her ability.

Having produced such a voluminous amount of various material, Angelou has said she once hoped to assemble some into one volume. She has picked out a variety of entries - *Ajax*; *Georgia, Georgia*, the screenplay; some of her short stories; a scenario of *All Day Long*, and bits and pieces done for *Playgirl* and the *New York Times*, to showcase a cross-section of her writings.[11] Unfortunately, for the followers of Angelou, this book has not come to fruition, and some of those works have fallen into obscurity.

Angelou, however, has never faded from the scene. She has remained in demand. Some recent television involvement includes interviews with Bill Moyers for a series on creativity and a long discussion with Jane Wallace regarding achievement. She has also currently produced lyrics for the musical *King: Drum Major for Love* and served as writer and host for a documentary series: *Maya Angelou's America: A Journey of the Heart*. This series was (done) in conjunction with Guy Johnson.

Because her creative activities in print form and in the various dramatic and visual mediums attracted considerable attention, many colleges have invited Angelou over the years to speak on their campuses. Without exception, these talks have been extremely well-received and many have been video taped for multiple showings. Her talks actually are "performances," presentations similar to the material and format in her play *And Still I Rise*. In these public appearances, it is Angelou's custom to read her poetry, tell stories, and encourage young people in the audience to pursue educational goals. In her segment on the PBS Bill Moyer's program, "The Face of Evil," (1988) she follows her campus format and leaves her audience to discover her message from innuendo, as is her want. She does little direct expository analysis about the concept of evil, again preferring the subtlety of the story-teller to the impact of the preacher.

After more than six decades of private and public experiences, Maya Angelou takes a look back in a tight little volume of essays, speculating on the vicissitudes of life as she has known it. This book, titled *Wouldn't Take Nothing For My Journey Now* (1993) favors us with a condensation of her philosophy of life. Angelou's collection "eloquently, gracefully and authoritatively waxes poetic, somber and sometimes silly,"[12] according to Sandra D. Davis. The title reflects Angelou's view of her life from this point in time. She realizes that the ups and downs, the tears and the laughter have brought her to what she is today. Her reflections upon vulnerability and accomplishment are meant to guide her followers along the trail of coping.

The twenty-four independent commentaries seem to be randomly presented. There is no obvious organizational structure, topically, chronologically, or geographically. The length of the comments or parables varies from a simple paragraph to some seven pages. Whatever it takes to make her point apparently determines Angelou's offering. The taut little note on jealousy, for instance, takes very little space to warn of the danger of too much of that which can add spice to life. On the other hand, six pages are devoted to the value of life as lived by the servant lady, Aunt Tee, as contrasted to the sterile, lonely existence of her wealthy employers. Angelou stresses creative and imaginative excursions in life regardless of position or money. Positive thinking and self-respect are treasured as buffers against many of the problems and hurts of life. A description of an unintended racial slight ends not with hatred, but with sorrow that two interesting people were artificially prevented from enjoying each other. A rather simple little tale about attire manages to leave a message regarding sensitivity to the feelings of others -- even the very young -- but still encourages one to be oneself.

There is an autobiographical tilt to the collection inasmuch as the entirety is based on personal experiences and observations that have led to specific conclusions by Angelou on life in general. This is not, however, a book of autobiography. It is rather words to live by: something to consider in developing a personal coda. Angelou says here's what I have seen or done and learned and I would like you to gain from my perceptions. The broad swatch of topics rather brings to mind the jottings from a writer's journal. Death, love, faith, dignity, virtue, grace, womanhood, choices, all these weighty conditions are concisely addressed. Many personal vignettes support Angelou's conclusions, but other opinions expressed are those honed from life's living lessons. The dominant Angelou theme of people being more alike than unalike again emerges as the major message from this volume.

Something new can be found with each re-reading of *Wouldn't Take Nothing For My Journey Now*. Perhaps because of the brevity of the individual essays, the language is crisp and pointed. There is no room for excess verbiage. A precision is dictated by form. Angelou achieves this goal without obvious omissions. The musicality of the essays sways the soul and stimulates the mind. Maya Angelou summarizes and distills Maya Angelou for all willing to listen.

Notes

[1]Jeffrey M. Elliot, *Conversations with Maya Angelou* (Jackson, MS: University Press of Mississippi, 1989) 34.

[2]Elliot 72-3.

[3]Elliot 13.

[4]Peter Bailey, *New York Times Film Review 1971-72*, March 26, 1972, (New York: New York Times and Arno Press, 1973) 242.

[5]A. H. Weiler, *New York Times Film Review 1971-72* (New York: New York Times and Arno Press, 1973) 233.

[6]Donald Bogle, *Blacks in American Films and Television* (New York, Garland Publ. Co., 1988) 89.

[7]Elliot 34.

[8]Michael Arlen, "The Air," *The New Yorker* 14 May 1979: 157.

[9]Donald Bogle 320.

[10]Donald Bogle 346-7.

[11]Elliot 67.

[12]Sandra D. Davis, "Maya Angelou Makes Journey Worth Taking," *News-Press*, Dec. 26, 1993, p. 3F.

Chapter 6

Abstracts in Ethics

No analysis or review of the autobiographies of Maya Angelou can fail to include a discussion of the moral objections being raised by some groups. In fact, *I Know Why the Caged Bird Sings*, lauded by many as a literary classic which should be read and taught to all African-American young people is one of the ten books most targeted for exclusion from high school and junior high school libraries and classrooms. This puts Angelou in honored company since Mark Twain and John Steinbeck are also on the list. Angelou's vivid style, including realistic language and reprehensible activities have made *Caged Bird*, and *Gather Together in My Name* volumes subject to censorship. This threat to First Amendment rights is particularly dangerous at a time when young people are aware of the hypocrisy of society but left uninformed about their choices.

Throughout her life, Angelou has been exposed to wise sayings-- Mother Wit, maxims; and warnings to live by which gave her a code of understanding and an underlying stability that enabled her to withstand injustices and to evaluate the morality of the world in which she lived. Basic to interpretation and formulation of this code is the intense religious training of her African-American churches. Her writings attempt to pass these philosophical and theological perceptions along to others.

The code she verbalizes, however, at times appears to run contra to universal Christian-Judaic norms of ethics and morality. Many readers question the moral center advocated by Angelou as lacking condemnation of acts generally considered undesirable. Situational interpretations seem to affect Angelou's judgments and provide justification for acceptance of some unseemly actions. Angelou's messages, though clearly meant to create positive impressions for African Americans, can be perceived as condoning illicit and illegal activities. A wrong righted by another wrong only demonstrates two wrongs, nothing right. An early vignette in *Caged Bird* (92-3) notes a Mrs. Cullinan demeaning Angelou by deliberately and regularly misnaming her. The young Marguerite retaliates by breaking some favorite china of the lady's. This leaves us with two wrongful acts which may satisfy the perpetrators but from which comes no real good. Neither party turns the other cheek nor apologizes for being hurtful which might be the civilized "good" response. The acceptance of tit for tat does not show a developed sense of morality and both actions deserve condemnation. The child's glee is understandable but cannot be left without censure. This incident passes as worthy of praise but many righteous souls would be indignant if this were used as a lesson in self-esteem. The revenge motif cannot enhance character. This is unacceptable comedy since both parties are guilty of unthinking stereotypical behavior.

The major event in *Caged Bird* that draws comment is the rape sequence. There are objections raised because of the realistic language employed in a detailed description of the happening. The morality of the affair and its ultimate resolution are questionable for many, and particularly as a picture suitable for young people. It has a particular value, however, to some critics who see a warning for the very young and a lesson to them as to choices they can make. By recalling the incident fully, Angelou manages to indict the action while still referring to the rapist as not entirely an ogre. The real lack of moral judgment arises from the vigilante style of justice exercised without recrimination when the perpetrator is brutally killed by person or persons unknown. Angelou herself by retreating into silence assumes a portion of unwarranted guilt and demonstrates a moral confusion. This double crime, the rape and the murder, does not present a case of right versus wrong. The rapist was deserving of punishment for a heinous offense, but when tried and freed by the court of law, that justice system should prevail, not to be considered wrong and arbitrarily readjudicated by injured parties. The ethics and morality that promote anarchy should not be held acceptable in a civilized society. The resolution of this event is unsatisfactory as a moral lesson. It equates with lynching which most certainly must be rejected on moral and humane levels by a society ruled by law. In *Caged Bird*, Angelou vigorously objects to a white sheriff's ready acceptance of white lawlessness as well as his assumptions about blacks: "His confidence that my uncle and every other Black man who heard of the Klan's coming ride would scurry under their houses to hide in chicken droppings was too humiliating to hear" (*CB* 14-15).

Maya Angelou sometimes steps out of chronological character in her autobiographies to make statements or tell stories that reflect situational ethics. In *Caged Bird* she repeats a lengthy, folklore story (the Red Leg tale) about some blacks who con wealthy bigoted whites. These whites are guilty of having bilked many blacks. This and similar tales were told by friends of Daddy Clidell to instruct Angelou, to protect her against victimization. The revenge motif again suggests that the two wrongs can make something right, contrary to any statutory laws or justice other than that which might be generated on the streets. While this type of story appears in the folklore of many cultures, it should not be accepted as ethically correct to cheat another person to get even. This again is a lesson with no saving grace, just saving face. Angelou remarks, "It wasn't possible for me to regard them as criminals or be anything but proud of their achievements. . . . The needs of a society determine its ethics . . . " (*CB* 190). This stance has been questioned as to its efficacy as a moral and ethical model.

Another comment in *Caged Bird* reported that " . . . law violations are weighed on a different set of scales in the Black mind than in the white" (*CB* 190). This thesis has reappeared regarding a predominately minority jury charged with determining guilt or innocence in a highly publicized murder trial. The influences of reality do not justify such interpretations of good or evil. Excusing recognized illegal or immoral behavior does not cleanse it or sanitize it. People must still be aware of and responsible for their actions. An orderly, reasonable, and healthy society could not exist under such assumptions. Morality cannot be judged by anything other than universally established standards of right or wrong, good or evil. Even at the cost of denying ethical correctnesss of common practices in the African-American society and condemning the survival-at-all costs theme, Angelou would perhaps better serve her people by denouncing blatantly illegal activities and responses. She clearly knows the difference and speaks of survival with style, not survival by any means. This is shown by her statement that it was hard to think of life in

St. Louis where "Prohibition, gambling and their related vocations were so obviously practiced it was hard for me to believe that they were against the law" (*CB* 51), even knowing all such were illegal. Young readers looking to *Caged Bird* for direction might be misled toward acceptance of these illegalities, thus the negative reaction of some critics.

The moral determinations espoused by Maya Angelou in her writings and her public comments reflect the influences of all factors of her life experiences. She draws from what she has known and what she has been told to be true. She seems to try to find accomodation for diverse ethical or moral stances such as those of Momma Henderson and Mother Vivian. Momma tolerated the taunts of the white-trash youngsters, turning to a hymn, whereas Vivian made fools of the insulting whites at the Fresno Desert Hotel. Neither woman is demeaned. Momma turns the other cheek, showing superiority; while Vivian takes a stand which gives her an upper hand. Both responses were morally correct and though diametrically different delivered the same lesson.

Despite condemnation of racism and slavery throughout her writings, labeling them absolute evils, Angelou abandons her absolutes in favor of moral relativism. It would seem a position of absolutes would be more favorable for one who has personally endured discrimination. An ultimate evil cannot be a limited evil, even if mitigating circumstances are present. However, Angelou accepts limited evils in some circumstances. In a long interview in 1977, she says that what is morally acceptable in a society depends on society's culture. For example, prostitution may be condemned viciously in our society, but condoned as a natural means of survival in another. Con men prey upon the greedy and thus are not despised by those with whom she grew up. The victims deserve their fate. Angelou also chastizes those blacks who forget their poverty-stricken, downtrodden background and take on a white middle-class morality which serves them poorly and unsuitably.[1]

Here, Angelou condemns those who moralize on the basis of values which are not their own. A society's acceptance of prostitution, which like racism is another form of dehumanization, does not mean that prostitution is ever morally permissible, regardless of its cultural tolerance. The practice of selling youngsters into prostitution and the custom of mutilating the clitoris of millions of women, although acceptable in some countries, would seem contrary to our own moral code. Just because someone is greedy does not mean that he can be taken advantage of without culpability; a con man should not be admired. Angelou's criticism of blacks taking on the morality of middle-class whites overlooks the fact that acceptable moral behavior of any established ethnic group in America at least gives lip-service to honesty, fairness, truthfulness, loyality, integrity, and responsibility. These are not white values nor black values; nor are they poor values nor rich values; they are values, valid with all peoples, even if practiced hypocritically. Angelou adds to this list her personal admiration of the virtues of courage and courtesy.[2] She praises these attributes in many of her interviews and public speeches. These are qualities considered highly desirable by most societies. The civility of a society is enhanced and maintained by observance of these attributes. All humanity relies upon such interactions. Fringe "values," although operational in forced, undesirable situations, condone stealing, dishonesty, lying, vandalism, and irresponsibility and are not values at all. They are justifications for expedient living. All ethical people reject and condemn these actions as disruptive and destructive of trust in society and strive to rise above a level which supports such behavior. All people deserve to be treated with dignity and are expected to respond with dignity, not advantageously.

Some Angelou detractors have posited that the frequency of comments and anecdotes relating racial discrimination occurrences throughout her writings create an "apologia" for those who would justify actions outside the accepted norms. They contend that racial pride should emphasize accomplishments in mainstream life, the Ralph Bunches, the Colin Powells, etc. There is a majority of African Americans who live middle class lives and are offended by the stereotypes advanced by the visible criminal activities of a very small minority of their brothers. Current research places the lawbreakers at around four percent.

Angelou never really defines morality. She proposes that for the first time since the early nineteenth century, whites have expressed a moral concern by questioning the Watergate activities.[3] Watergate was about breaking and entering and subsequent lies, actions meriting condemnation, but certainly not the first or only moral lapse addressed by the public. Down through the years, constitutional amendments such as voting rights for women and anti-trust legislation have attempted to correct some major moral oversights. Angelou knew that there was considerable preaching in the South of a strong Christian morality which in practice was often violated. Hypocrisy has always been a condition of mankind. But this does not invalidate the general consensus of the virtue and desirability of a standard code of moral conduct meant to create limits on social behavior. This credo must be ascribed to by all civilized beings. Some voices objecting to *Caged Bird* and its subsequent books find the moral lessons presented therein short of a generally supported creed. They would prefer stronger stands for moral guidance. However, *Caged Bird* is not meant to be taken as a behavioral bible. It is an entertainment whose messages are open to interpretation. It is expected that religion provides a moral center for its followers. Angelou allows religion to be more of a social influence in her writings. Her God is a good and forgiving God rather than a stern and judgmental figure. Selwyn Cudjoe and others hold that "religion is designed to keep the Afro-American in an oppressed condition."[4] Angelou joyfully embraces religion and finds its music and services personally vitalizing and unifying for a black community."[5] In an interview, she has expressed her gratitude for the presence of a God in her world.[6] She rejects the idea that religion kept blacks subjugated and docile. She contends that blacks go to their churches not from a sense of duty but because it is a totally different and unique world. The joy of religious involvement provides a sharing of all the human emotions -- amusement, sadness, happiness and the excitement of life itself.[7,8] The social structure and interactions, the behavioral examples, are of greater import and more memorable than the preacher's sermon as told in Angelou's writings. These messages carry a positive cultural impact.

Angelou sometimes seems to confuse values with taste. Values "express approval or disapproval; that is, some action, or belief is right or wrong, good or bad . . . . "[9] They are regulatory by nature. Taste suggests a liking or preference for something. Some perceived values are simply expressions of tastes, of likes and dislikes. And there cannot be any substantive dispute about taste; it is individual. The appreciation of music is a societal value, but preferring one kind of music over another is an individual taste. Despite an ongoing mantra that stresses people are more alike than unalike, Angelou has been quoted railing at those who want everyone, blacks, Mexican Americans, Asisans or whomever, to be just like whites. She feels that an acceptance of modus vivendi amongst people could bring harmony.[10]   But modus vivendi, as generally used, refers to matters of taste. It is like a style of dressing and does not necessarily express a moral value. For people to want African Americans to be like whites in taste is offensive and arrogant, but wanting anyone to practice moderation toward each other is a proper value. The promotion of a value system protecting societal norms does not negate the importance of any segment of that society, nor limit its unique tastes.

Angelou does advocate universal socially acceptable values in her writings through the teachings of her grandmother Henderson and her own instructions to her son. Those objecting to loose morality in her work are overlooking the strong guidance also incorporated. Her awareness of the realities of life does not suggest embracing antisocial actions. It is easy to confuse forgiveness with tolerance. Rising above the degradation and humiliation forced upon some human beings by those of lesser ethical behavior is a message stressed by Maya Angelou. She still holds out the carrot of a just and peaceful life. By example, she keeps alive hope for redemption and acceptance. Her positive optimism allows opportunity for sinners as well as angels to strive for justice and a better life. Angelou's moral critics overlook her obligation and desire to inform, enlighten, and perhaps inspire many who are forced to live on the edge of righteousness. The exercise of censorship closes minds and blocks desires to rise out of the limitations of poverty and injustice.

Notes

[1] Jeffrey M. Elliot, ed. *Conversations with Maya Angelou* (Jackson, Mississippi: University Press of Mississippi, 1989), 82-83.

[2] On the *Talking With David Frost* show (1995), Angelou said, "The greatest of all virtues is courage." There is no question that this is a highly admirable quality. An interesting counter example, however, is Napoleon's comment about the importance of courage in combat. "The first quality of a soldier is constancy in enduring fatigue and hardship. Courage is only second. Poverty, privation and want are the school of the good soldier."

[3] Elliot 23.

[4] Selwyn Cudjoe, "Maya Angelou and Autobiographical Statement," *Black Women Writers 1950-1980*. ed. Mari Evans (New York: Anchor Books/Doubleday, 1984), 6-24.

[5] Elliot 87.

[6] Elliot 143.

[7] Elliot 202, 203.

[8] Elliot 203.

[9] Annette T. Rottenberg, *Elements of Argument* (New York: St. Martin's Press, 1982), 31.

[10] Elliot 43.

Chapter 7

Overview: "And So It Was Written"

Carl Jung, the psychologist, suggested that the human personality can be divided into a four-sided figure -- the "quaternity." The complete woman, according to Jung, has four dominant stages: virgin, spouse, mother, and wise woman. Angelou's success with her writings may be attributed to an adherence, whether conscious or unconscious, to this Jungian "quaternity" of goddesses. These archetypal characteristics readers intuitively recognize and accept. In her autobiographies, Angelou herself exemplifies the four stages: she is a young virgin until she questions and explores her sexuality; she is a spouse, having been married three times; she is a devoted mother to her son, diligently squiring him to manhood; and she is a wise woman by virtue of absorbing the wisdom of her elders and lessons of life. Her autobiographical journeys carry her through these four stages ending with the worldly-wise, mature Angelou ready to face life anew in the land of her birth. She is responding to the Negro spiritual urging her to "Fly Away Home" -one journey completed, another to begin. Angelou often ends her anecdotes with commentary that enhances the narrative, that offers a rationale for understanding the event. She provides closure, which keeps her audience focused and comfortable with her interpretations. Angelou handles a fairly lengthy agenda in her five autobiographical books and in her poetry. Her wit and word sense have crafted some good reading.

Many of her stories involve her experiences as a black female trying to survive in a white dominated world, a world that displaced her and that made her sometimes feel "worthless," even when she was succeeding. Angelou's reaction to what she sees as a collective negative feeling toward African Americans is the rationale for her protest against the ugliness of racial injustice. "It was awful to be Negro and have no control over my life" (*CB* 153). Uppermost in Angelou's mind throughout her five books appears to be her desire to disabuse readers of unfair categorizing, unfair stereotyping, and to develop a positive posture. She demands an openness of mind by whites and blacks. Vivian tells her, "We can't change because the whites won't change." She praises the so-called Uncle Toms and Mammys who silently suffered to survive, but denounces the movie images who project stylized ignorance.

Angelou tries to emphasize the importance of family: immediate, extended, or acquired. She rejects the myth that the African-American family is fragmented and missing. Being a successful mother is of prime concern to her. It is important that African-American children grow up to be responsible men and women of character despite the ugliness of racism they may endure. Throughout the adventures written about her life, Angelou always has worked hard and carved her niche through talent and determination. She has willingly exposed herself to criticism and proven a match for her critics.

Psychologists recently have been publishing reports on repressed rage, its causes and effects. In addition to racial

discrimination and segregation, Angelou had been subjected
to classic causes: abandoment by her father and mother
while a youngster, assumed guilt from her traumatic rape,
and frequent displacement. Angry assessments of white
power and difficulty in choosing faithful male partners may
have been direct results of her inner rage. It required years
of seasoning to come to terms with her personal devils.
She does deal directly with her rage in *Caged Bird* and by
so doing exorcises that demon. Her books reflect a gradual
tolerance developed toward whites. *Caged Bird* is caustic
in tone toward white society while *All God's Children Need
Traveling Shoes* is much softer and accepting of others.
She praises many black males throughout her writings, but
seems to reconcile to their failing her. We are all products
of our cumulative experiences and our responses are tailored
by these without conscious realization. In contrast to
repressed rage, suppressed rage can present a healthy aspect.
Suppression implies an awareness and a control, whereas
repressed anger is deeply buried in the psyche and exerts its
influence surreptiously. Moving into the suppressive mode
shows a strength and courage both of which are attributes
admired and demonstrated by Angelou.

Sometimes Angelou's anecdotes of her experiences read
like trite theatrical world tales. There is an accumulation of
insight, but not as obvious as that found in another
classical narrative: James Weldon Johnson's *Autobiography
of an Ex-Colored Man*, where he details a step-by-step
discovery of himself. In Angelou, the self-discovery
process is intertwined with a discovery of the world and
appears to offer only small bits of introspection and
self-examination. These characteristics seem to be more a
part of a sub-text and are buried in the travels and
adventures. An example of this would be a paragraphs
relating Angelou's emotional responses to the slave prison

in Ghana and to the village of Dunkwa (*AG* 97-105). This approach supplies a framework that makes her books seem light and easy to read. Angelou cleverly imbeds her messages and clearly addresses the problems of her people and herself without being stiffly structured or pedantic.

Angelou's references to the spectrum of human love reinforce the humanity of those who people her books. They are depicted as full and equal with all other human beings. Their pure emotions are not subject to racial restrictions. The diverse cast of characters is an important component of the writings of Maya Angelou. Through them Angelou can emphasize black pride. Despite being "caged" by "prejudice, illogical hate and Black lack of power," her folklore proudly sings of courage, humor, resourcefulness, integrity, survival, determination, and a black identity.

Caged Bird might have ended with the black national anthemn sung at the close of the eighth-grade graduation ceremony. White educational leaders indicate a continuing segregation, but the black audience replies with,

> Lift ev'ry voice and sing
> Till earth and heaven ring
> Ring with the harmonies of Liberty . . . (*CB* 155)

The irony of these words leaves to future years the song that says "We Shall Overcome."

Maya Angelou has *publicly* overcome the "slings and arrows of outrageous fortune." Her writings and performances chronicle her triumphs. Her words cry out her message of awareness. Her students and her audiences realize the intelligence, the resilience, the strength, and the moral purpose of this remarkable woman.

The impact of her writing has resulted in her gaining

academic recognition as a visiting professor at several universities. She was a lecturer at the University of California in 1966, a writer in residence at the University of Kansas in 1970, and also in 1970 she was a Chubb Fellow at Yale. In 1974, she served as Distinguished Visiting Professor at Wichita State University; California State University, Sacramento; and Wake Forest University. In 1982 she received her lifetime appointment to Wake Forest. The open atmosphere of Wake Forest welcomed Angelou and provided her with a secure operational base. She is a regular guest lecturer at colleges throughout the country and appears on television periodically.

Angelou has received many awards. She holds over 25 honorary doctorates. In 1975 she was given the *Ladies' Home Journal* "Woman of the Year Award in Communications." In 1977 she earned the Golden Eagle Award for her documentary on Afro-Americans in the Arts for PBS. In 1983 she received the Matrix Award in the field of books from Women in Communications, Inc. She was appointed by President Gerald Ford to the Bicentennial Commission, and by President Jimmy Carter to the Commission of International Women's Year. She is a pioneer female member of the Screen Directors Guild and is on the Board of Trustees of the American Film Institute. In 1986 she was selected to tour with a Fulbright group to Ghana. She is a member of the Advisory Board for the Oklahoma Project for Discourse and Theory.[1,2] In 1990 she received the Candace Award, and in 1993 the Horatio Alger Award. Also in 1993, President Bill Clinton commissioned her to write and present a poem at his inauguration. The 1994 Horatio Alger Award ceremony found her reading a new poem especially created for that occasion. The 1995 Million Man March called upon her talent.

With a life time of publicly living as an African

American, from her own chronicles of a segregated childhood and accelerated adolescence to responsible maturity, Angelou, cloaked in honors and recognition brings before the entire world on the day of the inauguration of a Southern president, this strong woman created by her own efforts. The very public person with her humor and dignity, speaking on behalf of all people, recites as the voice of all Americans, her own words of hope and unity, "On the Pulse of the Morning." The familiar image, from lecture halls, television screens and stages, delivers poetry of her creation in the rhythms of her heritage. In a rich firm voice, Maya Angelou again performs. She has earned her recognition, her space, her niche in a Southern, mostly white university where her freedom of speech and action symbolize what can be achieved by perseverance, hard work and a good bit of courage. It is brave to share your life in print.

Maya Angelou wrote a series of autobiographies and established herself as a poet. She will not be bested by life. "All my work, my life, everything is about survival. All my work is meant to say, 'You may encounter many defeats, but you must not be defeated.'"[3] Angelou seems determined to get the best she can from life and with her words and actions inspire others to do the same. Her books are her testimonials. They contain a litany of oppression but show to the world Angelou's ability to survive with at least a modicum of style and faith.[4] She emerges from the stifling confines, the "caging" of discrimination, to her place as a "Phenomenal Woman."

Notes

[1]"Maya Angelou," *Current Biography* (New York: H. W. Wilson & Co., 1974) 12-15.

[2]"Maya Angelou," *Contemporary Authors* (Detroit: Gale, 1987) 21-24.

[3]Jeffrey M. Elliot, *Conversations with Maya Angelou* (Jackson, Mississippi; University Press of Mississippi, 1989), 152.

[4]Elliot 15-16.

Postscript

The influence of Maya Angelou has increased in recent times and it would appear that her messages will be secured for future generations. She is widely embraced as a source of wit and wisdom for both blacks and whites.

Her sermons of reconciliation are broadcast far and wide. Her message of alikeness does not fall on deaf ears and her soothing comments serve to heal perceived differences amongst those who listen.

Her life will long shine on dark corners and illuminate a path to the unity of mankind.

Bibliography

1. *Books by Maya Angelou*

Autobiographies

I Know Why the Caged Bird Sings. New York: Random House, 1970; London: Virago, 1984.

Gather Together in My Name. New York: Random House, 1974; London: Virago, 1984.

Singin' and Swingin' and Gettin' Merry Like Christmas. New York: Random House, 1976; London: Virago, 1985.

The Heart of a Woman. New York: Random House, 1981; London: Virago, 1986.

The Aristocrat. Newton, Iowa: Tamzunchale Press, 1986. Excerpted from *I Know Why the Caged Bird Sings.*

All God's Children Need Traveling Shoes. New York: Random House, 1986; London: Virago, 1987.

Children's Literature

Mrs. Flowers: A Moment of Friendship. Minneapolis, MN: Redpath Press, 1986.

Life Doesn't Frighten Me. Painting by Jean Michel Basquiat New York: Stewart Tabori and Chang, 1993.

My Painted House, My Friendly Chicken, and Me. Photographs by Margaret Courtney-Clarke. New York: Clarkson Potter, Inc., 1994.

Essay

Wouldn't Take Nothing For My Journey Now. New York: Random House, 1993.

Poetry

Just Give Me a Cool Drink of Water 'fore I Diiie. New York: Random House, 1971; London: Virago, 1988.

Oh Pray My Wings Are Gonna Fit Me Well. New York: Random House, 1975.

And Still I Rise. New York: Random House, 1978; London: Virago, 1986.

Shaker, Why Don't You Sing. New York: Random House, 1983.

Maya Angelou Poems. New York: Bantam, 1986.

Now Sheba Sings the Song. With Tom Feelings. New York: Dutton, 1987; London: Virago, 1987.

I Shall Not Be Moved. New York: Random House, 1990; London: Virago, 1990.

On the Pulse of the Morning. New York: Random House, 1993.

The Complete Collected Poems of Maya Angelou. New
  York: Random House, 1994.
Phenomenal Woman. Four Poems Celebrating Women.
  New York: Random House, 1994.
A Brave and Startling Truth. New York: Random House,
  1995.

2. Plays, Screenplays and Television (Produced)

"Cabaret for Freedom" (musical revue), 1960.
"The Least of These" (two-act drama), 1966.
"Blacks, Blues, Black" (ten one-hour programs), National
  Educational Television, 1968.
"Georgia, Georgia" (Film), 1972.
"Ajax," adapted from Sophocles' play (two-act drama),
  1974.
"All Day Long," American Film Institute, 1974.
"And Still I Rise" (one-act musical), 1976.
"The Legacy" (Afro-American Television Special), 1976.
"The Inheritors" (Afro-American Television Special), 1976.
"I Know Why the Caged Bird Sings," with Leonora Thuna
  (Film), 1979.
"Sister, Sister" (drama) NBC-TV, 1982.

3. Recordings

"Miss Calypso" songs, Liberty Records, 1957.
"The Poetry of Maya Angelou," GWP Records, 1969
"Maya Angelou," Center for Cassette Studies, 1974.
"Maya Angelou Talks About Her Life, Her Mother and
  Grandmother and Various Influences, 1976.
"Maya Angelou," Tapes for Readers, 1978, 1979.

"Maya Angelou," An Interview. Tapes for Readers, 1979.

"Women in Business," University of Wisconsin, 1981.

"Maya Angelou," Minneapolis Public Library and Information Center, 1981.

"Maya Angelou the Writer/the Person." Nebraska ETV Network for the Nebraska Educational Television Council for Higher Education, 1981.

"Maya Angelou, " PBS Video, 1982, 1987.

"Maya Angelou Takes Interviewer, Bill Moyers, Through Her Small Town in Rural Arkansas," 1986.

"Maya Angelou at HSU," 1986.

"Maya Angelou Speaks at Russell Sage," 1987.

"Maya Angelou," "The Faces of Evil," Filmed in Chicago and Dallas with Bill Moyers. Public Affairs Television. WNET/New York, 1988.

"Maya Angelou, African American Artist." History on Video, 1989.

"Maya Angelou," ICA Video, 1989.

"Maya Angelou Lecture," History on Video, 1990.

4. Uncollected Articles

"Cicely Tyson: Reflections on a Lone Black Rose." *Ladies' Home Journal* (February 1977): 40-46.

"Why I Moved Back to the South." *Ebony* 37 (Feb. 1982): 130-4.

"Save the Mothers." *Ebony* 4 (Aug. 1986): 38-39.

"Why Blacks Are Turning To Their Southern Roots." *Ebony* 45 (April 1990): 44.

5. *Bibliography*

Cameron, Dee Birch. "A Maya Angelou Bibliography." *Bulletin of Bibliography* 36, 1 (Jan/March 1979): 50-52.

6. *Interviews*

Angelou, Maya, and Carol E. Neubauer. "Interview," *The Massachusetts Review*, Summer 1987, 286-92.
Elliot, Jeffrey M. *Conversations with Maya Angelou*. Jackson, MS: University Press of Mississippi, 1989.
Redmond, Eugene J. "Boldness of Language and Breadth: An Interview with Maya Angelou." *Black American Literature Forum* 22 (Summer 1988): 156-57.
Thomas, Arthur E. "Interview with Maya Angelou." *Like It Is. Arthur E. Thomas Interviews Leaders on Black America*. New York: Dutton, 1981.

7. *Critical Works about Angelou*

Arensberg, Liliane K. "Death as a Metaphor of Self in *I Know Why the Caged Bird Sings*," *College Language Association Journal*, December 1976, 273-91.
Bertolino, James. "Maya Angelou is Three Writers: *I Know Why the Caged Bird Sings*." in *Censored Books*, ed. Nicholas J. Karolides, Lee Burress, and John M. Kean. (Metuchen, N.J: The Scarecrow Press, Inc. 1993), 299-305.
Bloom, Lynn Z. and Ning Yu. "American Autobiography; The Changing Critical Canon," *a/b: Auto/Biography Studies*, 9:2 (Fall 1994): 167-180.
Braxton, Joanne M. *Black Women Writing Autobiography*.

(Philadelphia: Temple University Press, 1989), 181-201.

Braxton, Joanne M. "Maya Angelou" in *Modern American Women Writers* ed. by Elaine Showalter. (New York: Scribner's, 1991), 1-8.

Buss, Helen M. "Reading for the Doubled Discouse of American Women's Autobiography," *a/b: Auto/Biography Studies*, 5:1 (1991): 95-108.

Cordell, Shirley J. "The Black Woman: A Focus on 'Strength of Character' in *I Know Why the Caged Bird Sings*." *Virginia English. Bulletin* 36 (1986): 36-39.

Cudjoe, Selwyn. "Maya Angelou and the Autobiographical Statement." *Black Women Writers*, ed. Mari Evans. (New York: Anchor Books/Doubleday, 1984) 6-24.

Demetrakopoulos, Stephanie A. "The Metaphysics of Matrilineism in *Women's Autobiography*." Women's Autobiography, ed. Estelle C. Jelinek. (Bloomington: Indiana University Press, 1980.) 180-205.

Dundes, Alan, ed. *Mother Wit from the Laughing Barrel* (Engelwood Cliffs, N. J.: Prentice-Hall, 1973.)

Egan, Susanna. *Patterns of Experience in Autobiography.* (Chapel Hill, N.C.: University of North Carolina Press, 1984.)

Estes-Hicks, Onita. "The Way We Were: Precious Memories of the Black Segregated South." *African American Review* 27, 1 (Spring 1993) 9-18.

Georgoudaki, Ekaterini. "Contemporary Women's Autobiography; Maya Angelou, Gwendolyn Brooks, Nikki Giovanni, Lillian Hellman, and Audre Lorde." *Diavazo*, 237 April 1990: 62-69.

Fleming, Margaret and Joe McGinnis, eds. *Portraits: Biography and Autobiography in the Secondary School.* Urbana, Illinois, NCTE, 1984.

Fox-Genovese, Elizabeth. "Myth and History: Discourse of Origins in Zora Neale Hurston and Maya Angelou."

Black American Literature Forum. Vol. 24, No. 3 (Summer 1990): 221-235.

Freeman, Sharon. *Voice Youth Advocates* 9 (Aug/Oct 1986): 170.

Froula, Christine. "The Daughter's Seduction: Sexual Violence and Literary History." *Journal of Women in Culture and Society* 11, 4 (1986): 621-644.

Georgoudaki, Ekaterini. *Race, Gender, and Class Perspectives in the Works of Maya Angelou,* Gwendolyn Brooks, Rita Dove, Nikki Giovanni, and Audre Lorde. (Thessaloniki: Aristotle U. of Thessaloniki, 1991).

Gilbert, Sandra. "A Platoon of Poets." Poetry (August 1976): 290-297.

Gilbert, Susan. "Maya Angelou's *I Know Why the Caged Bird Sings*: Paths to Escape." *Mount Olive Review* (1987): 39-50.

Gruesser, John C. "Afro-American Travel Literature and Africanist Discourse." *Black American Literature Forum,* 24, 1 (Spring 1990): 5-20.

Hiers, John T. "Fatalism in Maya Angelou's *I Know Why the Caged Bird Sings.*" *Notes on Contemporary Literature* 6, 1 (1976): 5-7.

Hughes, Langston and Arna Bontemps, eds. *Book of Negro Folklore.* (New York; Dodd, Mead, 1958).

Jelinek, Estelle C. "Introduction; Women's Autobiography and the Male Tradition." *Women's Autobiography,* ed. Estelle C. Jelinek. (Bloomington: Indiana University Press, 1980): 1-20.

Jones, Jimmy. "Author's Memory of Stamps: Total Segregation." *Arkansas Gazette* 19 July 1970: B 1-3.

Kent, George E. "Maya Angelou's *I Know Why the Caged Bird Sings* and Black Autobiographical Tradition." *Kansas Quarterly* 7 (1975): 72-78.

Kinnamon, Keneth. "Call and Response: Intertextuality in Two Autobiographical works by Richard Wright and Maya Angelou." *Belief vs. theory in Black American Literary Criticism.* ed. Joe Weixlmann and Chester J. Fontenot. Greenwood, FL: 1986. 121-134.

Lionnet-McCumber, Francoise. "Autobiographical Tongues: (Self-) Reading and (Self-) Writing in Augustine, Nietzsche, Maya Angelou, Marie Cardinal, and Marie-Therese Humbert." Diss. University of Michigan, 1986.

Lupton, Mary Jane. "Singing the Black Mother: Maya Angelou and Autobiographical Continuity," *Black American Literature Forum* 34, 3 (Summer 1990): 257-276.

MacKethan, Lucinda H. "Mother Wit: Humor in Afro-American Women's Autobiography. *Studies in American Humor* 4 (1985): 51-61.

McCall, Cheryl. "Maya Angelou." *People* 8 Mar. 1982: 92-97.

McMurry, Myra K. "Role Playing as Art in Maya Angelou's 'Caged Bird,'" *South Atlantic Bulletin*, May 1976, 106-11.

McPherson, Dolly. *Order Out of Chaos. The Autobiographical Works of Maya Angelou.* (New York: Peter Lang, 1990).

Mayfield, Julian. "Black on Black, A Political Love Story." *Black World* (Feb 1972): 55-71.

Moore, Opal. "Learning to Live: When the Bird Breaks from the Cage. In *Censored Books*, ed. by Nicholas J. Karolides, Lee Burress, and John M. Kean. (Metuchen, N.J.: The Scarecrow Press, Inc., 1993), 306-316.

Neubauer, Carol E. "Displacement and the Autobiographical Style in Maya Angelou's *The Heart of a Woman.*" *Black American Literature Forum* 17

(1983): 123-129. A report on The Heart of a Woman.

O'Neale, Sondra. "Reconstruction of the Composite Self: New Images of Black Women in Maya Angelou's Continuing Autobiography." *Black Women Writers*, ed. Mari Evans. (Garden City, N.Y.: Anchor/Doubleday, 1984.) 25-36.

Pascal, Roy. *Design and Truth in Autobiography.* Cambridge: Harvard University Press, 1960.

Ramsey, Priscilla R. "Transcendence: The Poetry of Maya Angelou." *Current Bibliography on African Affairs.* Amityville, NY.: Baywood Publishing, 1984-1985, 17, 2: 139-153.

Rowe, Anne. "Maya Angelou." In *American Women Writers*, ed. Lina Mainiero. (New York: Frederick Ungar, 1979.)

Schultz, Elizabeth. "To be Black and Blue: The Blues Genre in Black American Autobiography." *Kansas Quarterly* 7 (1975): 81-96.

Stepto, R. B. "The Phenomenal Woman and the Severed Daughter." *Parnassus Poetry in Review* 8 (Fall/Winter 1979): 312-20.

Vermillion, Mary. "Reembodying the Self: Representations of Rape in *Incidents in the Life of a Slave Girl* and *I Know Why the Caged Bird Sings. Biography* 15, 3 (Summer 1992): 243-60.

Index

A

Abrahams, Roger D., 47,48
Adams, Phoebe, 74, 82
Aldan, Daisy, 3, 99
Allen, Woody, 17
Almeida, R. E., 94
Angelos, Tosh, 88-89
Angelou, Maya (Marguerite Johnson,
    'Ritie)
    academic recognition and
    awards, 162; and humor, 27,
    29-30, 38, 59, 114; as storyteller,
    30, 32; confrontations, 10, 80,
    104; love of languages, 91; on
    autobiography, 4, 16; on poetry,
    119-120, 133; personal growth, 7,
    79, 83, 86, 91, 95; protest, 8,
    72, 79, 92, 99, 133, 159; purpose
    of writing, iii, iv, 23, 77;
    relationship to black autobio-
    graphy, 5, 8, 23, 110; word use,
    ii, 19-20, 22, 37, 45, 46, 53, 103,
    111, 121, 131; work ethic, 8, 37,
    133

WORKS—BOOKS, AUTOBIOGRA-
PHIES (Chronologically)
    *I Know Why the Caged Bird
    Sings*, 1, 2, 6, 13-18, 22-23,
    28, 30-35, 37-39, 41-47, 49,
    53, 54-73, 137-138, 142, 148-
    152, 154-155, 159-161
    Gather Together in My Name, 2,
    35, 39, 53, 72, 73-86, 126,
    142, 148
    *Singin' and Swingin' and Gettin'
    Merry Like Christmas*, 3, 53,
    87-95
    The Heart of a Woman, 3, 35,
    53, 96-107
    *All God's Children Need
    Traveling Shoes*, 3, 7, 28,
    53, 107-114, 160

WORKS—BOOKS, ESSAY
    *Wouldn't Take Nothing for My
    Journey Now*, 3, 23, 145-146

WORKS—BOOKS, POETRY
    And Still I Rise, 111
    I Shall Not Be Moved, 118, 133
    Just Give Me a Cool Drink of